goof-proof

BUSINESS WRITING

D1365248

goof-proof
BUSINESS
WRITING

Lauren Starkey

LearningExpress ®

NEW YORK

Library of Congress Cataloging-in-Publication Data:
Starkey, Lauren B., 1962-
    Goof-proof business writing / Lauren Starkey.
        p. cm.
Includes bibliographical references.
    ISBN 1-57685-464-7 (pbk.)
    1. Business writing. 2. Commercial correspondence. I. Title.
HF5718.3.S73 2003

                                   2003000421

Printed in the United States of America

9 8 7 6 5 4 3 2 1

First Edition

ISBN 1-57685-464-7

For more information or to place an order, contact LearningExpress at:
    900 Broadway
    Suite 604
    New York, NY 10003

Or visit us at:
    www.learnatest.com

ABOUT THE AUTHOR

Lauren Starkey is a writer and editor, specializing in educational and reference works, with over 10 years of experience. For eight years, she worked on the *Oxford English Dictionary*, and she is the author of *Certified Fitness Instructor Career Starter* and *Hotel/Restaurant Management Career Starter*. In addition, she has coauthored several career-related books.

CONTENTS

SECTION FIVE

The Goof-Up—Not Understanding the Basic Mechanics of Writing

SECTION SIX

The Goof-Up—Confusing the Types of Business Writing

INTRODUCTION

Even if you have the education and experience necessary to get a good job, inadequate writing skills could hold you back. Why? Because you need good writing skills to convey your knowledge and experience. Poor written communications can make you appear less competent than you are, and keep your ideas from getting the audience—and the praise—they deserve.

Learning how to write in a clear, organized, and error-free manner is what *Goof-Proof Business Writing* is all about. In the following chapters, the basics of good writing, from organization to mechanics, are broken down into 50 simple Goof-Proof Rules. Follow them, and you will be led step-by-step toward better workplace communications.

• HOW THE GOOF-PROOF METHOD WORKS •

The 50 Goof-Proof Rules are presented in Goof-Up form. You will read about a common mistake, then learn how to Goof-Proof yourself, or avoid the mistake. *Goof-Proof Business Writing* covers everything you need to know to improve your writing:

- how to organize your thoughts
- targeting your audience and writing to them
- knowing what you want to say and saying it clearly
- using the right format for you communication
- choosing the right words to get your point across

Writing well also means following the rules of grammar and spelling. Although most business communications are written on a computer with grammar and spell checks, these high-tech helpers aren't goof-proof. You still need to know the basic mechanics in order to write well. The five Goof-Proof Rules of mechanics will explain simply and directly the information you need to know.

The book is divided into seven sections, each covering a different writing topic:

- Section One explains the importance and how-to's of organizing your ideas, and writing effective introductions, bodies, and conclusions.
- Section Two teaches you how to write directly to your audience by understanding who they are and giving them the right amount of information.
- Section Three is all about clarity. Determine exactly what you want to say and how to say it in the most direct, specific, and unambiguous way.
- Section Four explains the importance of word choice. You will learn how to correctly use the most confused and misused words, and how to avoid alienating or baffling your audience through improper word choices.
- Section Five gets back to basics. The parts of speech and common grammatical errors are explained, and made Goof-Proof. Spelling, punctuation marks, and capitalization are also covered.
- Section Six shows you eight of the most common business writing formats, and how to use them correctly. You will learn how to write agendas, letters, e-mails, memos, reports, instructions, and proposals, and see samples of each.

- Appendices: Finally, find more grammar, spelling, and writing resources, along with information on how to take full advantage of your computer's formatting, grammar, and spelling tools.

As you read *Goof-Proof Business Writing*, remember that your written communications say a lot about you. If they are poorly organized, full of spelling mistakes, or use offensive language, you will appear less than professional, and whatever you have to say will probably be lost in the confusion. Don't allow your business reputation to suffer because of poor grammar or word choice. Writing well is a skill that can be acquired at any time, and is made simple in this Goof-Proof book.

After using this book and mastering the **Goof-Proof Rules**, your writing will improve. You will know how to get right to the point, using the right words and the right format. And your workplace audience will appreciate your efforts—you are writing to busy people, who don't have time to figure out what you are trying to say. By getting it right the first time, your ideas and efforts will be rewarded with understanding, and your professional image will improve, too.

goof-proof

BUSINESS WRITING

THE GOOF-UP:
DISORGANIZED WRITING

Good business writing begins with organization. Even the shortest e-mail benefits from time spent developing your ideas. *Prewriting* or brainstorming becomes even more important when you are writing something longer, such as a report, involving a variety of issues and ideas. The notes taken during the prewriting stage should then be transformed into an outline, which helps set the direction of your writing. Finally, before you write, organize your information logically.

Remain organized during the writing process. Follow your outline, using it to write a topic sentence and then a strong introduction. In the body of your communication, bring up all of the relevant points you organized earlier, and conclude by leaving your reader with a firm understanding of your subject, argument, or analysis. Adhere to the etiquette of business writing by using appropriate headings and conclusions in all of your letters, memos, reports, and even e-mails.

RULE #1: Spend Time Prewriting

There are two simple steps to Goof-Proof prewriting: determining the purpose of your communication and exploring your subject on paper.

● GOOF-PROOF IT! ●

Before you begin writing, specify these three things:

1. the action of your message
2. the object of that action (the what)
3. the receiver of that action (the who)

Then, write down all of your ideas about the *what* that you believe the *who* should know.

To prewrite effectively, answer four key questions. You might want to set up four columns on a piece of paper, one each for purpose, action, object of the action, and receiver of the action. Or, you may prefer to simply jot down the questions and answers:

1. What is the purpose of my writing?
2. What is the action?
3. What is the object?
4. What/who is the receiver of the action?

This table shows a few simple examples of the four-column method of determining your writing goal.

PURPOSE	ACTION	OBJECT OF THE ACTION	RECEIVER OF THE ACTION
welcome the new employees	to welcome		the new employees
explain the new policy	to explain	the new policy	employees
report a violation of procedures	to report	violation	management

Once you've come up with a goal, get your ideas down on paper. They can be in the form of a neat list, moving from the most to least important, or they can be random, needing more organization later.

● GOOF-PROOF RULE OF THUMB ●

Logic and organization aren't important in prewriting. The goal is to be thorough. Explore your subject on paper, toss out ideas, identify points to be made, and consider arguments in favor of—or even against—your point of view.

● GOOF-PROOF SAMPLE ● PREWRITING NOTES

In this example, the subject has been asked by his boss to write a memo about a recent meeting they both attended. He needs to explain the important details to the rest of his department. Before writing the memo, he makes a list of ideas for possible inclusion.

Department needs more manpower—
    Management considering hiring two assistants
    Who would use new assistants?
Last two presentations not accepted by clients—why?
    Not enough time to come up with good material?
    Client not specific about what she wanted ahead of time?
New graphic software not being used by everyone in Creative
    Department—
    Too time consuming to learn?
    Many prefer old software?
    Too difficult to master?

RULE #2: Choose an Appropriate Organization Method

Make sense out of your prewriting notes by using a method that is appropriate to your subject and the purpose of your writing.

● GOOF-PROOF IT! ●

Here are five proven organizing strategies for your notes:

1. Order of importance: Rank supporting ideas from most important to least important, or vice versa.
2. Chronological: Organize your ideas in the order in which they did happen or will happen.
3. Cause and Effect: Explain what happened (cause) and what happened as a result (effect), or vice versa.
4. List: Create a roster of items of equal importance.
5. General to Specific: State supporting details, then the main point, or vice versa.

● GOOF-PROOF SAMPLE ● SPECIFIC TO GENERAL ORGANIZATION

Shakira is an excellent employee, and deserves a raise.
hasn't had pay increase for 2 years
no sick days taken
works well with others
regularly meets or exceeds individual production goals
volunteers to help others

RULE #3: Transform Prewriting into an Outline

Never waste prewriting work—organize it logically into a working outline by creating major and minor topics.

● GOOF-PROOF IT! ●

Creating an outline begins with a reading of your prewriting notes. First, group related ideas together, looking for major topics (which can be headings), and minor ones (which can be subheadings, examples, or details).

Start by defining your major points, and rearrange them until they make sense and follow a logical progression. You will be able to see the relationships between your ideas as you outline them and determine their importance (major point, minor point, example, or detail). If you need more supporting details or facts—subcategories—you can add them now.

● GOOF-PROOF RULE OF THUMB ●

As you outline your information, use topics, which are one-word or short phrases, or write out full sentences for each point on your outline.

● GOOF-PROOF SAMPLE ● STANDARD OUTLINE

A standard outline form using Roman and Arabic numerals and upper and lower case letters looks like this:

I.
   A.
   B.
      1.
      2.
         a.
         b.

• GOOF-PROOF SAMPLE •
NOTES TRANSFORMED INTO OUTLINE FORM

These are notes taken by a senior account representative during a meeting with a client.

At meeting: Marge L., Larry D., Lily M., Jeremy V.
Ideas for expanding company product list
- Marge: must appeal to a younger demographic
- Jon: will research trends online

New benefits program
- New HMO
- Free dental coverage for all employees

New incentive plan
- Holiday bonuses

Objectives: everyone will come up with five ideas for the next meeting

Here are the same notes organized into an outline that describes the senior account representative's understanding of the facts after meeting with a client.

  I. Overview

    A. List meeting attendees

    B. New product ideas

       1. Appeal to younger demographic

       2. Research trends

  II. Discussion of Topics

    A. New benefits program

       1. New HMO

       2. Free dental coverage for all employees

    B. New incentive plan

       1. Holiday bonuses

  III. Business Objectives

RULE #4: Use Appropriate Headings and Salutations

Business writing is all about fitting in. Standard headings and salutations should be used at all times.

● GOOF-PROOF IT! ●

For **business letters**, a standard heading includes (in this order):

- writer's address
- date
- recipient's address
- re: or subject line
- salutation

● GOOF-PROOF CHECKLIST ● BASIC GUIDELINES FOR SALUTATIONS OR GREETINGS

✓ Begin with the word "Dear."
✓ If you are not on a first-name basis with the reader, use Mr./Ms./Mrs. and the reader's last name (*Dear Mr. Jones*).
✓ If you are on a first-name basis, use his or her first name (*Dear Janine*).
✓ If you don't know the reader's name, use his or her title (*Dear Customer Service Representative*).
✓ If you don't know the reader's gender, use Mr./Ms. ___ (*Dear Mr./Ms. Jones*).
✓ Follow the salutation with a colon (:).

For **memos**, a heading is used without a separate salutation. It should include these five parts, in order:

1. to
2. from
3. date
4. re: or subject line
5. cc

● GOOF-PROOF SAMPLE ● MEMO HEADING

To: M. Kaur
From: E. Sicalowski
Date: September 15, 2003
Re: Sample Acquisition
cc: D. Thomas, W. Wei

For **e-mails**, there is no need to create a separate heading because all e-mail software creates headings automatically. Heading information includes the subject line you provide, the recipient, the sender, and the date. Never leave out a subject line, and always follow the salutation guidelines for letters. If you are writing to a business associate who is also a friend, his or her name followed by a comma or colon is appropriate.

RULE #5: Write a Strong Introduction

Especially important for longer letters and memos, an introduction prepares your audience to hear what you have to say.

● GOOF-PROOF IT! ●

Begin by writing a topic sentence, based on your prewriting goal and the major points of your outline. Then, determine whether you intend to argue a point, explain or present your subject, or analyze your subject.

If you are *arguing* a point, your introduction should state your claim in a topic sentence, give some of the explanations and evidence you will present, and give an order to your argument.

● GOOF-PROOF SAMPLES ●
ARGUMENTATIVE INTRODUCTORY SENTENCES

Product A has been a best seller for our company for the past three years, but we should spend the resources necessary to create Product B.

Although the team wants to keep it on our calendar, the meeting scheduled for next Tuesday will not help us meet our objectives if the client does not attend.

● GOOF-PROOF RULE OF THUMB ●

An introduction has three purposes:
1. to tell the reader what the communication is about (the subject)
2. to let the reader know what you think, feel, or know about that subject (the main idea)
3. to catch the reader's attention (so he or she actually reads what you wrote)

If you are *explaining* your subject, your introduction will mention the types of information you will use, and the order in which you will present them. Your topic sentence will clearly state your subject.

● GOOF-PROOF SAMPLES ●
DECLARATIVE INTRODUCTORY SENTENCES

- Our company has conducted extensive research to determine that there are many reasons why product A will become a best seller.
- Regular meetings with our clients keep us focused on our goals and them informed as to our progress, according to a number of important sources.

If you are *analyzing* your subject, you will explain in your introduction the breakdown of your analysis, and how you will present it.

● GOOF-PROOF SAMPLES ●
ANALYTICAL INTRODUCTORY SENTENCES

- I have studied the data available, and determined that we need to provide more breaks to those working in manufacturing.
- Our last four meetings with Client C were unproductive for a number of reasons.

RULE #6: Use the Body of Your Writing to Present Supporting Information

Explain your subject, analyze it, or argue for it, using your outline as your guide.

• GOOF-PROOF IT! •

Here is where you argue your point, analyze your subject, or explain your ideas. Follow through with whatever you have raised in your introduction, giving your reader details, examples, and/or analysis.

The body of your communication is the most straightforward part to write. Simply follow your outline by including all relevant topics and supporting information. If you feel you need more examples or a stronger explanation, you can add them in as you write, or go back to your outline and rework it with the new information before proceeding.

• GOOF-PROOF SAMPLE • BODY PARAGRAPHS

Here is an outline followed by the body of a memo written from it. Note that the memo paragraphs contain all of the facts about the dress code.

I. New Dress Code for All Employees

   A. begins on September 1

   B. shirts

      a. no T-shirts

      b. no sleeveless shirts

   C. pants

      a. no shorts

      b. no jeans

      c. no athletic attire

    D. skirts/dresses

        a. no miniskirts

        b. no denim

    E. shoes

        a. no sandals

        b. no flip-flops

        c. no sneakers

    F. consequences of violating dress code

        a. first offense: verbal warning

        b. second offense: written warning and 30-day probation period

        c. third offense: dismissal

    G. attached announcement must be distributed

Please inform everyone in your group that the new dress code for all employees will take effect on September 1. All employees will be required to wear professional business attire while in the office. In this context, professional business attire excludes T-shirts, sleeveless shirts, shorts, jeans, athletic attire, miniskirts, sandals, flip-flops, and sneakers.

Violations of the new dress code will be handled as follows: A verbal warning will be given after the first offense, a written warning and 30-day probation period after the second offense, and a third offense will result in dismissal.

If any employees have any questions about the parameters of the dress code, they should contact Martin Lamb in Human Resources immediately to schedule an appointment.

RULE #7: End with an Effective Conclusion

Leave your reader with a firm understanding of your subject, argument, or analysis, and a good impression of your writing.

● **GOOF-PROOF IT!** ●

Your communication is not considered complete without a conclusion. Think of every business document as an essay, and remember that the 'A' essays in school always wrapped up nicely in the end.

● **GOOF-PROOF CHECKLIST** ● **STRATEGIES FOR CONCLUSIONS**

Note the example given after each strategy that demonstrates how it can work.

✓ Summarize or restate the main idea. This works best with longer texts.
    Once again, thank you for your help.

✓ Make recommendations. This is a particularly useful conclusion for reports.
    Moving forward, I think we should keep track of . . .

✓ Look to the future. What do you anticipate doing or accomplishing?
    I look forward to working with you on this project.
    I hope to complete this inventory by Thursday.

✓ Use a call to action. Tell your readers what they should do.
    Call Ximena no later than Tuesday, August 1, if you will attend.
    Please respond by Friday, January 16.
    Fill out the attached form and return it as soon as possible.

✓ Provide a reference person for readers to contact with questions or for more information.

> If you have any questions, please don't hesitate to call me at extension 333.

> Please call AnneMarie in Accounting for more information.

✓ Thank your readers for their time or for what you're asking them to do.

> Thank you for your prompt attention to this matter.

> Thank you for your time.

> I appreciate your time and effort.

✓ Remind readers why this matter is important to them.

> Remember, we cannot process your overtime sheets without a supervisor's signature.

● GOOF-PROOF SAMPLE ●
CONCLUSION

Here is a conclusion that uses strategies 1, 2, and 7. Some of the points made in the introduction are restated, and an explanation is given for what is at stake. An action is also recommended (distribution of an attached announcement).

> It is important that employees understand the seriousness of this policy. Management based its decision to implement it upon evidence that casual dress codes lead to a decrease in productivity. Our new dress code will help to maintain the reputation and integrity of our company by keeping us aware of the need for professionalism. Please distribute the attached announcement immediately.

RULE #8: Use an Appropriate Closing

Follow the rules of business writing to the very end of your communication by signing off with the right type of closing.

● **GOOF-PROOF IT!** ●

Decide how formal your communication is, and then choose the appropriate closing. The following list of closing words and phrases is ranked in order of formality, with number 1 being the most formal (as well as the most commonly used in business writing):

1. Sincerely
2. Very truly yours
3. Yours truly
4. Sincerely yours
5. Cordially
6. Best regards
7. Regards
8. Best
9. Yours

● **GOOF-PROOF RULE OF THUMB** ●

If you are writing a letter, your conclusion will end with your signature, preceded by a closing word or phrase. If you are writing a memo, your name appears at the top of the page, in the heading, so never close with your signature.

● **PUTTING IT ALL TOGETHER** ●

Effective business writing needs organization; the longer your communication is, the more organization you need. Take time to think through your subject, exploring a variety of details, examples, or arguments that will illuminate or strengthen it. Organize the best and most pertinent information in an outline that clearly spells out your writing plan.

When you're done outlining, you will have a visual tool to guide you through the writing of the introduction, body, and conclusion of your work. The time spent preparing will make the writing process easier, and the final product more successful.

• GOOF-PROOF GUIDELINES •

Remember these guidelines for organizing your writing:

- Spend time prewriting, or gathering your thoughts and ideas.
- Transfer prewriting notes into outline form.
- Organize information logically.
- Write a strong topic sentence and introduction that tells the reader where you are going.
- Follow your outline as you work on the body of the communication.
- Leave your reader with a thorough understanding of your subject, restating it if necessary.
- Always take time to write a clear and concise conclusion.
- Use appropriate headings and closings.

section **TWO**

THE GOOF-UP:
BEING UNAWARE OF YOUR AUDIENCE

Writing should always be audience specific: What you say and how you say it depends entirely on to whom you are saying it. This means that before you begin to write, you need to know your audience. The more you know about your reader, the better you will be able to write to him or her. That means anticipating your audience's needs and expectations, and tailoring your communication to meet them.

Before you begin writing, take some time to find answers to the following questions:

- Who will read your communication?
- Why should they read it?
- What special needs or characteristics does this reader or group of readers have?

RULE #9: Adapt Your Writing to Deal with Multiple Audiences

If your audience is made up of a number of people with varied backgrounds, don't try to write to all of them at once.

● GOOF-PROOF IT! ●

Technically referred to as writing to the *lowest common denominator*, assuming that none of your audience knows anything puts you at risk of boring the most knowledgeable while enlightening the least knowledgeable. However, assuming that your audience knows something it doesn't is also an inadequate strategy.

There are two effective strategies for writing to multiple audiences:

1. Divide your communication into sections. Each section should be written to a segment of your audience, and be clearly labeled with headings and introductions so that groups can find the information they need, while skipping over what they don't need.
2. Consider using attachments if there is background information you need to supply for some, but not all, of your audience.

● GOOF-PROOF SAMPLE ●
WRITING TO MULTIPLE AUDIENCES

Memorandum
To: All Employees
From: The Partners
Date: September 16, 2003
Re: Using Grammar Check Function

It has come to our attention that a number of recently filed briefs contain many grammatical errors. Not only do these errors take away from our professional reputation, but some of them confuse the meaning of the arguments in which they are found.

If you are already familiar with the grammar check function on your laptop, and have it activated as a default setting when starting a new document, skip to section three of this memo. Section three explains our new policy of having all briefs proofread by our librarian or a member of her staff before filing.

If you do not currently use grammar check, read section two for instructions on how to use it.

RULE #10: Learn about Your Audience

The better you know your recipients, the more details you will have to help you tailor your communication directly to them.

• GOOF-PROOF IT! •

As you begin thinking about your audience, consider the following questions. Depending on the importance of your communication, you may want to spend some time investigating the answers to one or more of these questions.

- What is the reader's level of authority? (For example, can he or she act on your letter, or will it have to be referred to someone else?)
- How does the reader prefer to be addressed? (Ms., Dr., Professor?)
- What is your work relationship? (Is he or she your boss or your subordinate? Are you friendly with one another?)
- What is the reader's age, gender, and present job?
- What is the reader's background (education, training, job experience)?
- What form of business communication does the reader use most (e-mail, formal letters, memos)?
- What type of business language is the reader accustomed to (technical lingo, medical lingo, legalese, etc.)?
- What does the reader expect to be included in your document? (For example, does he or she like every piece of information sent to him or her at one time, or would he or she rather see attachments later if at all?)
- Does the reader have a sense of humor?

● GOOF-PROOF RULE OF THUMB ●

When in doubt about your reader's preferences, it is usually better to err on the side of formality. If you make the mistake of writing a casual e-mail to someone who prefers more formal communications, the consequences will be much worse than if you write a formal letter to someone who prefers casual correspondence.

RULE #11: Establish a Positive Impression with Your Audience: Tone

Your audience will form an opinion about you based on a number of factors. The tone you use is important—make it positive to show you are confident and capable.

• GOOF-PROOF IT! •

Tone refers to the attitude you show both to your reader and about your subject. It can be friendly or cold, optimistic or pessimistic, confident or insecure. In any type of business writing, aim to convey a positive tone by:

- giving attention to what exists, rather than what is lacking
- focusing on the positive, rather than the negative
- conveying a confident and in-charge attitude

• GOOF-PROOF SAMPLES • POSITIVE AND NEGATIVE TONE

The following e-mails were written to gain admission to a workplace seminar. Note the difference in tone between the two.

Dear HR Rep:

I am interested in signing up for the seminar on morale in the workplace.

I know there are not many available spots, but I hope you will consider me, since I've been with the company for five years.

If you wish to contact me, you may call me at extension 111.

Kelly Guzman

Dear Hannah:

I just received your e-mail about the morale seminar. What a terrific idea! I'm certain that my group can benefit from this information. Please mark me down for a spot, and I'll mark my calendar.

Contact me at extension 222 to confirm.

See you next Thursday,

Kimberly Janey

In the first example, Kelly's tone is flat. She uses passive words such as *hope* and *wish*, which give the reader the impression that the writer isn't a person of action. She also points out the negatives, such as the space issue, and in her lack of enthusiasm, she all but asks to be excluded if there isn't enough space in the seminar.

Kimberly instead greets the sender by name, Hannah, and states that the seminar is a terrific idea—assuming that she will be a part of it. Her upbeat writing exudes confidence. She demonstrates action by asking for her place as well as by marking her calendar.

RULE #12: Establish a Positive Impression with Your Audience: Voice

Your audience will form an opinion about you based on a number of factors. Your use of the active instead of passive voice conveys energy and directness.

● GOOF-PROOF IT! ●

The *active voice* is simple and direct, one of the major goals of business writing. It connects an action with the person who is performing that action. The *passive voice* renders the *doer* of the action less obvious, if that person is ever identified at all.

Sentences written in the passive voice tend to be longer, and more difficult to understand. The active voice is concise and energetic, and it is the preferred writing style.

● GOOF-PROOF SAMPLES ●
ACTIVE AND PASSIVE VOICE

Active Voice: We suggest that you provide a written report.
Passive Voice: It is suggested that you provide a written report.

Active Voice: Let's schedule a phone conference for Thursday morning.
Passive Voice: A phone conference should be scheduled for Thursday morning.

Active Voice: Her assistant typed the letter.
Passive voice: The letter was typed by her assistant.

RULE #13: Choose Words with Your Audience in Mind

When you know to whom you are writing, you can use words to appropriately communicate with that person. Should you be casual or formal? Are you speaking for yourself or on behalf of a larger group?

● GOOF-PROOF IT! ●

Word choice refers to the degree of formality and activity you present in your writing. If you are communicating with your boss, you will be more formal than if you were writing to a close business associate. For example, you might use contractions (*you're, should've*) for the associate, but avoid them when communicating with your boss.

Using the first (*I* and *you*) rather than third-person (*she* and *he*) and active rather than passive language will make your writing more understandable and approachable. This is especially important if you have determined that your audience may have trouble understanding your point.

● GOOF-PROOF SAMPLES ● APPROPRIATE WORD CHOICE

The following examples were written by the same person, and both convey similar information. However, the first is written to a colleague, and the second is addressed to an entire law firm.

> Hey, Kate, did you hear that Natalie's been offered her own column? I'm so excited for her! Can't wait to read it next week. Her writing is always so funny and insightful.

Notice the informal, casual word usage—contractions, slang, first name greeting.

Please join us in welcoming our newest columnist, Natalie Chester, to our newspaper staff. Natalie has written several freelance pieces for us, and we know that she will be a wonderful addition to the team.

Notice the word usage—*our, we, us*—and the camaraderie in the tone of the announcement.

RULE #14: Use the Correct Format

Don't make the mistake of working hard on your writing, and then putting it in a format that is inappropriate. Your audience may never read the communication if its format puts them off.

• GOOF-PROOF IT! •

Formats change with audience, and convey levels of formality. Here are some general guidelines:

- E-mail: (short, without proper salutations) use to convey a small amount of information quickly. Some companies reserve e-mail use for those lower on the corporate ladder, while others permit electronic correspondence between all employees.
- Letters: (more formal, following stringent formatting rules) typically reserved for communicating with those outside your company.
- Memo: (less formal) appropriate for internal correspondence; not for those outside the company.

• GOOF-PROOF RULE OF THUMB •

Never send a letter in the body of an e-mail; instead, send it as an attachment. An e-mail should not exceed 12 lines of text.

• GOOF-PROOF SAMPLES • FORMATS

The following e-mail, memo, and letter samples address the same topic and are written by the same person but use different levels of formality.

Subject: Everlasting Eyeshadow
Date: Friday, November 29, 2003 09:00:02
From: Cristina Parson cparson@instantmakeover.com
To: Linda Ball lball@instantmakeover.com

Linda,

Our Everlasting Eyeshadow line is finally ready for distribution! I left a
sample of each color on your desk this morning. Let me know what you
think. Stunning Sophistication is my favorite, but I'm so proud of all of
them. I think our hard work really paid off.

Thanks,
Cristina

INSTANT MAKEOVER
Interoffice Memo

To: All Employees
From: Cristina Parson
Date: November 29, 2003
Re: Our Newest Product

Our Everlasting Eyeshadow line is ready for distribution. I'd like to thank
all of you for your work and input on this project. Samples of all colors
will be available for all employees on Monday.

Cristina Parson
Instant Makeover
305 West 50th Street, New York, NY 10004
(333) 555-1299
cparson@instantmakeover.com

November 29, 2003

David Stewart
Man-Made Manufacturing, Inc.
111 University Avenue
Trenton, New Jersey 12856

Dear David:

RE: Everlasting Eyeshadow

The samples you sent me yesterday exceeded our expectations. I'd like to thank you, as well as your entire team, for carefully and expediently handling all of the production issues associated with this product.

Yours truly,

Cristina Parson
CEO, Instant Makeover

CP/bp

RULE #15: Remember the Human Element

In today's technical age, it is more important than ever to personalize and warm up your messages. Aim to strike a balance between professional and friendly.

• GOOF-PROOF IT! •

Make your written words sound like you. Convey who you are professionally by using these guidelines:

- What would you like people to say about you, based on your writing? What qualities would you like them to see in you? Emphasize your positive traits (funny, caring, diplomatic, etc.) through your writing to create a classic, original piece.
- Refer to yourself as *I* to avoid sounding unnatural and stilted. You can also use the word *you*, but don't overdo it, or you will sound patronizing:

  Compare: Your work on the Letterman project was insightful, thorough, and right on target, Melanie.

  With: I think the whole office benefited from your work on the Letterman project, Melanie. It was insightful, thorough, and right on target.

- Use *We* when speaking for your whole company. If you have constant contact with a particular employee from another company, you may use *I*, but to convey a message that has the clout of your entire company, use *we*.
- Avoid colloquialisms, including slang. The *real you* can come up with something original, rather than relying on worn-out words and phrases.

● GOOF-PROOF SAMPLES ●
"COLD" AND "WARM" LANGUAGE

The following e-mails were sent to all employees in a company to alert them to a change with a client.

Cold: As of noon on Thursday, employees will need to address our largest client, XYZ Corporation, by its new name, YZ Incorporated. Any employees found violating this policy will not be offered overtime work for a period of five days following the violation.

Warm: As your Human Resources liaison, I am writing to inform you that management has requested that we all show respect for our largest client by using only their new name. The changes at XYZ Corp. were difficult for all involved, and we can show our sensitivity to this situation by referring to them only as YZ Incorporated after noon on Thursday.

Management has asked me to let you know that anyone who does not comply will not be offered overtime work for a period of five days. Your attention to this matter is greatly appreciated!

RULE #16: Understand Your Audience's Level of Understanding, and Write to It

Imagine your reader putting down a report you spent a week writing because she doesn't understand all of the jargon you used. Knowing that she works in a different field should have tipped you off that you needed to drop the jargon and write to your audience.

• GOOF-PROOF IT! •

When you know your audience, you know how much background information they might need, how technical you can get, and how familiar they are with the jargon in your field.

If you are writing to a fellow engineer who is familiar with your work, you can use as much technobabble as necessary to convey your point. If your audience works in a different field, however, you will need to slow down and explain yourself in greater detail, using language that is understood by all.

• GOOF-PROOF RULE OF THUMB •

If you have been working in your field for many years, you may have difficulty separating technobabble and jargon from plain English. When in doubt about word choice, choose the simplest option. Words classified as technobabble and jargon tend to have more syllables, prefixes, and suffixes than words typically recognized as plain English.

• GOOF-PROOF SAMPLE • LEGAL WRITING APPROPRIATE FOR A FELLOW LAWYER, AND A CLIENT

Lawyers and those in other professions with their own "language" need to be certain their message doesn't get lost when writing to an audience of non-lawyers. Compare these sentences:

A duty of care to the herein above mentioned plaintiff was breached by the defendant when the slippery floor was left unmopped by the defendant.

The defendant breached her duty of care to the plaintiff when she failed to mop the slippery floor.

● PUTTING IT ALL TOGETHER ●

Everything you write at work is meant to be read by someone else—your audience. Your purpose in writing is to convey information to that person or persons, with little or no chance that they will misunderstand, be alienated, or otherwise turned off by your communication. The best way to do that is to be aware of your audience throughout the writing process.

● GOOF-PROOF GUIDELINES ●

Remember these guidelines for organizing your writing:

- Writing at work is audience specific: What you say and how you say it depends entirely on to whom you are saying it.
- The more you know about your reader, the better you will be able to write to him or her, and successfully convey your information.
- Aim to convey a positive tone by giving attention to what exists, focusing on the positive, and sounding confident and in charge.
- Using the first (*I* and *you*) rather than third-person (*she* and *he*) and active rather than passive language will make your writing more understandable and approachable.
- Remember the human element in your business writing; strike a balance between sounding professional and being friendly.
- Use the appropriate format for your audience (e-mails are less formal; letters are more formal).
- Give your readers all of the information they need to fully understand your topic.

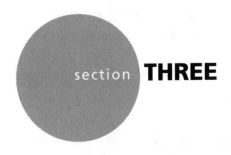

section **THREE**

THE GOOF-UP:
WRITING WITHOUT CLARITY

When writing for a business audience, you have one chance to reach your readers. They are busy people who won't bother spending time decoding your communications. That is why it is imperative that you say exactly what you mean as clearly and as quickly as you can.

Remember that your goal is to convey information. That goal won't be achieved if your readers don't understand your first few sentences or paragraphs, and stop reading, or if they finish reading but fail to grasp your message. Learning how to be a clear and accurate writer will help make your business communications successful.

RULE #17: Know What You Want to Say Before You Say It

When you are clear about your message, you can get right to the point.

● GOOF-PROOF IT! ●

Before you actually begin writing, take the time to clarify the point you are trying to make. The more precise you can be about exactly what you wish to achieve through your writing, the better you will communicate the information to your audience.

● GOOF-PROOF CHECKLIST ●

Follow these steps:

- ✓ Write down your overall goal for the communication.
- ✓ Read through your outline and circle, underline, or highlight your major points. Do they all support your goal?
- ✓ Brainstorm words and phrases that will accurately and concisely express those points (you may jot them down in the margin of your outline, or use a separate sheet).
- ✓ Use this list and your outline to guide your writing. Don't allow yourself to stray from your goal, or your major points.

RULE #18: Choose the Right Words

Well-chosen, specific words and phrases make your point clear.

● GOOF-PROOF IT! ●

Word choice is important when trying to make a point quickly and clearly. Using powerful adverbs and adjectives convey your ideas with punch, allowing you to say what you need to say in fewer words and with greater meaning. For example, *promptly* can take the place of *in a few days*; *productive* can take the place of *much was accomplished.*

● GOOF-PROOF LIST ●
POWERFUL, PRECISE ADJECTIVES AND ADVERBS

- directly involved
- unflagging dedication
- promptly accepted
- productive meeting
- hefty raise
- influential employee
- invaluable asset
- priceless decision

● GOOF-PROOF SAMPLES ●
VAGUE AND SPECIFIC SENTENCES

Here are some sentences that leave the reader guessing, followed by examples of how to be specific:

Vague: I hope to meet with you again soon!

Clear/Specific: We're looking forward to an answer about that contract by January 4.

Vague:	We greatly appreciated your help with the Randolph matter. You are a great new asset to our team.
Clear/Specific:	Your decision to renegotiate the Randolph contract earned us an additional $10,000. Pam and Ronan tell us you're the best new attorney on staff.

Vague:	Your investment should increase significantly by next year.
Clear/Specific:	Your investment should increase 10% by next year.

Vague	The new system has been very profitable.
Clear/Specific:	The new system has reduced operating costs by 30%.

Vague:	Our progress on this project is somewhat behind schedule.
Clear/Specific:	Our progress on this project is one week late.

RULE #19: Eliminate Ambiguity

Don't confuse your audience by using the wrong words, or by using the right words in the wrong order.

● GOOF-PROOF IT! ●

Ambiguous means having two or more possible meanings. The problem with ambiguous language is that the meaning understood by the reader may not be the one intended by the writer. This can be disastrous for business communications, which need to be absolutely clear. Here are two important guidelines to avoid ambiguity:

1. Refrain from using words and phrases with more than one meaning.
2. Be sure the words you use are in the right order to convey your intended meaning.

For example: *The photographer shot the model.*

This sentence can be read two ways: The photographer *shot* pictures with a camera, or the photographer *shot* the model with a gun. This kind of confusion can happen whenever a word has more than one possible meaning. *The photographer took pictures of the model* is a better sentence.

For example: *The woman ate the sandwich with a blue hat.*

Here, the *word order* of the sentence, not an individual word, causes the confusion. Did the woman eat her sandwich with her hat? Because the phrase *with a blue hat* is in the wrong place, the meaning of the sentence is unclear. Try instead: *The woman with a blue hat ate the sandwich.*

● GOOF-PROOF SAMPLES ●
CORRECTING AMBIGUOUS LANGUAGE

Ambiguous: When reaching for the phone, the coffee spilled on the table.

Clear: The coffee spilled on the table when *he* reached for the phone.

Ambiguous: I went to see the doctor with a severe headache.

Clear: I went to see the doctor because I had a severe headache.

Ambiguous: The famous artist drew stares when he entered the room.

Clear   The famous artist received stares when he entered the room.

Ambiguous: When writing on the computer, the spell checker often comes in handy.

Clear: The spell checker often comes in handy when I am writing on the computer.

RULE #20: Avoid Unclear Pronoun References

Pronouns should be used only when it is clear to whom they refer.

● GOOF-PROOF IT! ●

Another common mistake that interferes with clarity is the use of unclear pronoun references. (Pronouns, such as *me, you, he*, and *she*, replace nouns.)

For example: *I went to the meeting with Ted and Fred, and we took his car.*

Whose car? *His* could mean either Ted's or Fred's. The writer needs to use a proper name instead of the pronoun in order to eliminate the possibility the reader will not understand him or her.

Write instead: *Ted picked Fred and me up for the meeting, so we could all go together.*

For example: *They considered publishing the novel by the unknown writer.*

This is a common pronoun error: using a vague *they* when there are specific people behind an action, but the writer does not know exactly who those people are. Even without that information, you can revise it to be more precise:

A publishing company considered publishing the novel by the unknown writer.

• GOOF-PROOF SAMPLES •
UNCLEAR PRONOUN REFERENCES

Vague: *They* passed a new tax law yesterday.

Clear: *The State Senate* passed a new tax law yesterday.

Vague: Mr. Jones told Mr. James that he had found *his* missing report.

Clear: Mr. Jones told Mr. James that he had found *Mr. James'* missing report.

Vague: *They* closed the movie theater after they discovered several fire code violations.

Clear: *The owners* of the movie theater closed their doors after they discovered several fire code violations.

Vague: The police officer arrested the man after *he* attacked a sales clerk.

Clear: After the man attacked a sales clerk, *he* was arrested by a police officer.

RULE #21: Be Brief

Don't waste your reader's time by taking too long to convey your message.

● GOOF-PROOF IT! ●

Readers are quickly annoyed by ten sentences that express an idea that could have been stated in four or five. To be an effective writer at work, avoid using too many words when a few will do. There are a number of well-known (and well-used) words and phrases that should be eliminated from your writing because they aren't necessary, or should be altered to a shorter form.

The following are four of the worst offenders, with usage examples.

1. *Because of the fact that.* In most cases, just *because* will do.

   > *Because of the fact that* it rained, the game was canceled.
   > *Because* it rained, the game was canceled.

2. *That* and *which* phrases. Eliminate them by turning the idea in the *that* or *which* phrase into an adjective.

   > This is a manual *that* is very helpful.
   > This is a very helpful manual.

   > The meeting, *which* lasted five hours, ended at four.
   > The five-hour meeting ended at four.

3. *There is, it is.* These constructions avoid the direct approach and are often unnecessary. Instead, use a clear agent of action:

   > *It is* with regret that we must decline your kind offer.
   > We regret that we must decline your kind offer.

   > *There is* no reason we can find to disagree.
   > We can find no reason to disagree.

4. *That* by itself is a word that often clutters sentences unnecessarily, as in the following example:

> He said *that* he thought *that* the meeting was useful and *that* he was happy *that* there will be a follow-up meeting.
>
> He said he thought the meeting was useful, and he was happy there will be a follow-up meeting.

● GOOF-PROOF RULE OF THUMB ●
WORD CHOICES FOR CONCISE WRITING

Wordy:	Replace with:
a lot of	*many* or *much*
all of a sudden	*suddenly*
along the lines of	*like*
are able to	*can*
as a matter of fact	*in fact* or delete
as a person	delete
as a whole	delete
as the case may be	delete
at the present time	*currently* or *now*
basic necessity	*necessity*
both of these	*both*
by and large	delete
by definition	delete
compare and contrast	*compare*
due to the fact that	*because*
final destination	*destination*
for all intents and purposes	delete
has a tendency to	*often* or delete
has the ability to	*can*
in order to	*to*
in the event that	*if*
in the near future	*soon*
is able to	*can*
it is clear that	delete
last but not least	*finally*

on a daily basis	daily
on account of the fact that	because
particular	delete
period of time	period or time
somewhere in the neighborhood of	about
take action	act
the fact that	that, or delete
the majority of	most
the reason why	the reason or why
through the use of	through
totally obvious	obvious
with regard to	about or regarding
with the exception of	except for

● GOOF-PROOF SAMPLES ●
WORDY AND CONCISE SENTENCES

Wordy: The employees who were late missed the first set of awards.

Concise: The late employees missed the first set of awards.

Wordy: It is my feeling that we should hire her immediately.

Concise: I feel we should hire her immediately.

Wordy: I believe that there is the possibility that the manager who was recently hired is not too fond of me.

Concise: I believe the new manager may not be too fond of me.

RULE #22: Don't Repeat Yourself

Saying the same idea more than once wastes your reader's time. Get it right the first time, and move on.

• GOOF-PROOF IT! •

Another way to annoy or lose your reader is to state an idea or piece of information more than once. Writers repeat themselves unnecessarily because they are not sure that they have been clear, or they are not attentive to the need to be concise. Say it quickly and clearly the first time, and repetition won't be a problem.

For example:

Wordy:	We will meet at 4 P.M. in the afternoon.
Concise:	We will meet at 4 P.M.

P.M. means in the afternoon, so there's no reason to say *in the afternoon.* It's a waste of words and the reader's time.

• GOOF-PROOF SAMPLES • REPETITIVE SENTENCES

Wordy:	The room is red in color.
Concise:	The room is red.

Wordy:	It is essential that everyone arrive promptly and on time.
Concise:	It is essential that everyone arrive on time.

Wordy:	It's time to terminate the project and put an end to it.
Concise:	It's time to terminate the project.

Wordy:	The car that is gray in color must have been in an accident or collision.
Concise:	The gray car must have been in an accident.
Wordy:	Please let me know your plans as soon as possible and at your earliest convenience.
Concise:	Please let me know your plans as soon as possible.
Wordy:	Let's meet to discuss and talk through the client's wish list and desires.
Concise:	Let's meet to discuss the client's wish list.

● PUTTING IT ALL TOGETHER ●

Business writing is about communicating information. If that information doesn't make sense to your reader, or if it gets lost in poor writing, you haven't succeeded. Learn how to say what you mean clearly and quickly. Your audience will appreciate the time you spend on your writing.

● GOOF-PROOF GUIDELINES ●

Clear up your writing by following these Goof-Proof guidelines:

- The more precise you can be about exactly what you wish to achieve through your writing, the better you can communicate with your audience.
- Word choice is important when trying to make a point quickly and clearly. Using powerful adverbs and adjectives convey your ideas with punch.
- When writing for a business audience, keep in mind that you probably have one chance to reach your readers. They are busy people, and can't be bothered spending time trying to figure out what you mean.

- Avoid ambiguous language: Don't use words whose multiple meanings may cause confusion; be certain the order of words in your sentences conveys the meaning you intend.
- Check your pronouns: Is it absolutely clear to whom or what they refer?
- Don't use too many words when a few will do, and don't waste time by repeating yourself.

THE GOOF – UP:
CHOOSING THE WRONG WORDS

One of the best ways to accurately convey your ideas in writing (as well as speech) is to *choose the right words*. When you do so, your reader understands your intended meaning, and you achieve the goal of effective communication.

This sounds simple, and for the most part, it is. You already have a command of the English language that includes knowledge of thousands of words' denotative (literal) meanings. Therefore, all you need to do is choose the right ones to get your message across.

Saying what you mean, however, takes more than just an understanding of the *denotative* (literal, primary) meaning of a word. Many words have not just a *denotative* meaning, but also a *connotative* meaning. The connotation is a word's implied meaning, which involves emotions, cultural assumptions, and suggestions. Both meanings must be considered when making word choices.

Once you are certain of denotative and connotative meaning, you must consider whether the words you choose might offend or confuse your reader. That means being aware of inclusive language, proper levels of formality, and the often bewildering jargon of many professions. Business writing is about getting a message across. Always strive to do so without insulting, confusing, or annoying your audience.

RULE #23: Learn the Most Commonly Confused Words, and Use Them Properly

Commonly confused words sound or look similar, but have different meanings.

• GOOF-PROOF IT! •

Pay attention to the meaning of every word that you use in your writing. If you are unsure that the word you are using is correct, look it up in your dictionary (or refer to the list of commonly confused words below). When you misuse words, your writing suffers. One wrong word—using *illicit* when you mean *elicit*, for example—can completely change the meaning of an otherwise well-written letter. It can also result in making your reader question your intelligence.

The following list contains 20 of the most commonly confused word pairs or groups, along with a brief definition of each. If you recognize some of them as words you frequently confuse, jot them down and study them; you might want to make flashcards for each word, and use the cards to learn the definitions.

• GOOF-PROOF LIST •

CONFUSING WORDS	QUICK DEFINITION
accept	recognize
except	excluding
access	means of approaching
excess	extra
affect	to influence
effect (noun)	result
effect (verb)	to bring about

assure	to make certain (assure someone)
ensure	to make certain
insure	to make certain (financial value)
beside	next to
besides	in addition to
bibliography	list of writings
biography	a life story
complement	match
compliment	praise
decent	well-mannered
descent	decline, fall
desert	arid, sandy region
dessert	sweet served after a meal
disburse	to pay
disperse	to spread out
disinterested	no strong opinion either way
uninterested	don't care
elicit	to stir up
illicit	illegal
farther	beyond
further	additional
imply	hint, suggest
infer	assume, deduce
personal	individual
personnel	employees
principal (adjective)	main

principal (noun)	person in charge
principle	standard
than	in contrast to
then	next
their	belonging to them
there	in a place
they're	they are
who	substitute for he, she, or they
whom	substitute for him, her, or them
your	belonging to you
you're	you are

[QUIZ]

Do you know the difference between these confusing word pairs? Choose the correct word to complete each sentence. The answers can be found on page 173.

1. I *assured / ensured* Rebecca that her new hair-style was attractive.
2. *There / Their* sofa was delivered this morning.
3. The yellow dress fits better *then / than* the red one.
4. The *personal / personnel* office is in the back of the building.
5. To *who / whom* should I address this letter?

RULE #24: Learn the Most Misused Words, and Use Them Properly

There are a number of words that are misused frequently. Learn them so you won't misuse them.

● GOOF-PROOF IT! ●

Choosing the right words also means being aware of the many commonly misused ones. You may find examples of misused words in the media, on billboards and other signs, in speech, and in everyday writing. In fact, even when used incorrectly, these words often sound acceptable to many writers. Take the time to learn their denotative meanings, and avoid an embarrassing goof-up.

● GOOF-PROOF LIST ●

WORD	WHEN TO USE IT
amount	used when you cannot count the items to which you are referring, and when referring to singular nouns.
number	used when you can count the items to which you are referring, and when referring to plural nouns.
anxious	nervous
eager	enthusiastic, or looking forward to something
among	used when comparing or referring to three or more people or things
between	used when comparing two people or things
bring	moving something toward the speaker
take	moving something away from the speaker

Goof-Proof Hint: Remember, bring *to*, take *away*.

can	used to state ability
may	used to state permission
each other	when referring to two people or things
one another	when referring to three or more people or things
e.g.	an abbreviation for the Latin "exempli gratia," meaning *free example* or *for example*
i.e.	an abbreviation for the Latin "id est," meaning *it is* or *that is*
feel bad	used when talking about emotional feelings
feel badly	used when talking about physical feelings
fewer	when you can count the items
less	when you cannot count the items
good	an adjective, that describes a person, place, or thing
well	an adverb, that describes an action or verb
its	belonging to *it*
it's	contraction of *it is*

Goof-Proof Hint: Unlike most possessives, *its* doesn't have an apostrophe.

lay	the action of placing or putting an item somewhere; a transitive verb meaning something you do *to* something else
lie	to recline or be placed (a lack of action); an intransitive verb meaning it does not act on anything or anyone else
more	used to compare one thing to another.

Goof-Proof Hint: one of the two things compared can be a collective noun, such as *the ballplayers* or *the Americans.*

most   used to compare one thing to more than one
                      other thing.

that   a pronoun that introduces a restrictive (or
                      essential) clause
which   a pronoun that introduces a non-restrictive (or
                      unessential) clause

Goof-Proof Hint: Imagine a parenthetical *by the way* following the word *which.* "The book, which (by the way) Joanne prefers, is her first novel," is incorrect. "Lou's pants, which (by the way) are black, are made of leather," is correct.)

[*QUIZ*]

Choose the correct word to complete each sentence. The answers can be found on page 173.

1. My brother was being indecisive, so I was forced to decide *among / between* the two movies.
2. After working long hours for three months, Joan was *eager / anxious* to start her vacation.
3. I lost the game but didn't *feel bad / feel badly* because I'd tried my best.
4. Exhausted, she went to her bedroom to *lay / lie* down.
5. The dinner *that / which* we ate last night was delicious.

RULE #25: Don't Use Words That Aren't Really Words

It doesn't matter how often they are used, the words mentioned in this rule are not considered standard English and should never be used.

● GOOF-PROOF IT! ●

This rule is the easiest one to follow. Learn this list and always avoid using these words in your writing.

● GOOF-PROOF LIST ●

acrrosed/acrost: The adverb and preposition *across* has only one form; it never ends in the letter t.

alot: Incorrect spelling of *a lot;* often seen in informal writing, but should not be used in business or other formal writing.

anyways: Speech dialect form is not acceptable in written English; use *anyway*.

anywheres: Speech dialect form is not acceptable in written English; use *anywhere*.

brang/brung: Often seen masquerading as the past tense of *bring*; *brought* is the only correct past tense of *bring*.

everywheres: Speech dialect form is not acceptable in written English; use *everywhere*.

hopefully: Most often heard as a substitute for *I hope*; as such it is not a word. "*Hopefully* I'll get an 'A' of the test" is an example of nonstandard English. What the writer means is "I hope I'll get an 'A' on the test." *Hopefully* is a word, however, when used as an adverb to mean full of hope. For example: They waited *hopefully* for the firefighters.

irregardless: This blend of *irrespective* and *regardless* has been in use for about a century, but is still not considered a word in standard written English.

majorly/minorly: *Major* and *minor* are adjectives; these substandard forms are attempts to use the words as adverbs. Other words, such as *somewhat*, should be used instead.

nowheres: See *anywheres*.

somewheres: See *anywheres*.

theirselves/themself: Both are incorrect forms of *themselves*; because *them* is plural, *self* must be as well. Also, *their* combined with *selves* is incorrect because it suggests possession.

[QUIZ]

Rewrite the following sentences in standard English. The answers can be found on page 174.

1. He brang a calculator with him to the calculus final.
2. Hopefully the meeting will go well.
3. Anywheres you want to meet for lunch is fine with me.
4. Irregardless of the weather, we are going to play golf.
5. People should take responsibility for themself.

RULE #26: Don't Use Words or Phrases That Might Offend Your Reader

Whether or not its use is intentional, biased language can inflict harm on others. Always avoid bias in your writing.

● **GOOF-PROOF IT!** ●

It is imperative in business writing to avoid the use of biased language, including negative stereotypes, which may result in the exclusion or putting down of others. In your business writing, your goal is to include rather than to exclude. Understanding the purpose of inclusive language, and using it in your writing, will assure that your message gets across as intended, without causing offense. Replace any possibly offensive words and phrases with *inclusive language* that doesn't offend or degrade another person or group.

● **Types of Bias**

Gender
- Avoid the suffix *–ess*, which has the effect of minimizing the significance of the word to which it is attached (*actor* is preferable to *actress; proprietor* to *proprietress*).
- Do not overuse *he* and *him*. Instead, use *his* or *her* or *their* and *those;* or alternate between *him* and *her*.
- Degender titles. *Businessman* becomes *businessperson* or *executive; chairman* becomes *chair* or *chairperson; stewardess* becomes *flight attendant; weatherman* becomes *meteorologist*.
- When referring to a couple, don't make any assumptions. *Inappropriate:* Mr. Rosenberg and Caryn, Mr. and Mrs. Bill Rosenberg. *Appropriate:* Mr. Rosenberg and Ms. Fetzer.
- Use professional, rather than personal, descriptive terms. *Inappropriate:* Robin Benoit, a lovely associate. *Appropriate:* Robin Benoit, an experienced associate.

Race

- To avoid stereotyping, leave out any reference to race, unless it is requested by the individual, or is relevant to the subject of your writing, such as a report on the racial diversity in your company.
- Focus on a person's individual, professional characteristics and qualifications, not racial characteristics.

Disability

- Address the *person*, not their handicap.
- If your writing is specifically focused on disabilities or disease, or you must mention them for another reason, don't use words that imply victimization or create negative stereotypes. Terms such as *victim, sufferer, poor, afflicted*, and *unfortunate* should be omitted.
- Don't use *courageous* to describe a person with a disability unless the context allows the adjective to be used for all. *Successful* or *productive* work better in a business context.
- Always put the person ahead of the disability, as in *person with impaired hearing*, rather than *hearing-impaired person*.

[QUIZ]

Remove any biased language from the following sentences, and replace it with inclusive words or phrases. The answers can be found on page 174.

1. The chairman of our committee read a report regarding absenteeism among the waitresses.
2. Every employee must put personal belongings in his or her own locker.
3. The African-American tennis players Venus and Serena Williams are the best in the world.
4. Please support the efforts of our brave Vice President of Personnel, Dora Sinclair, by sponsoring her in the Relay for Life.
5. Did you send the invitation to Dr. Choe and Tannie?

RULE #27: Understand Positive and Negative Connotations to Choose Words Wisely

Connotative, or implied, meanings can be positive, negative, or neutral. Using a word without being aware of its implied meaning can offend your audience or make your message unclear.

• GOOF-PROOF IT! •

Connotation involves emotions, cultural assumptions, and suggestions. Some dictionaries offer usage notes that help to explain connotative meanings, but they alone can't be relied on when trying to avoid offensive or incorrect word choices.

For example, what feelings come to mind when you hear the words *skinny* or *thin*? *Skinny* has negative connotations, while *thin* is a more neutral selection. *Copy* or *plagiarize*? *Leer* or *look*?

If you were writing about a business retreat during which executives played favorite childhood games, you wouldn't choose the adjective *childish* to describe their behavior. *Childish* has a connotative meaning of immaturity, whereas *childlike*, a better choice, does not.

Similarly, the words *vagrant* and *homeless* have the same denotative meaning. However, *vagrant* connotes a public nuisance, whereas *homeless* suggests an unfortunate situation worthy of attention and assistance.

Imagine that you must write about a colleague's unfortunate experience with law enforcement. This episode was extremely embarrassing to your company, and you want to minimize its importance. You wouldn't say he was *busted*. This word has a connotative meaning of a violent overtaking of a criminal by the police. The term *arrest* is more neutral, whereas *police detention* sounds as positive as you can be with regard to a bad situation.

[QUIZ]

Do the following words have a positive or negative connotation?
The answers can be found on page 174.

1. inexpensive: positive / negative
2. encourage: positive / negative
3. aromatic: positive / negative
4. ludicrous: positive / negative
5. cozy: positive / negative

RULE #28: It Doesn't Always Pay to Be Wise

*No matter how often you see the suffix –*wise *in business writing, it is considered too informal, and should be avoided.*

● **GOOF-PROOF IT!** ●

The suffix *–wise* is defined as *in the manner or direction of,* (think of *clockwise, otherwise,* or *slantwise*). However, it is increasingly being used to mean *with relation to,* (think of *businesswise, tax-wise,* or *resourcewise*).

This use is considered informal, and although it has made it into buzzword status, it doesn't belong in business writing. Instead, try removing *–wise* from the noun, and adding the phrase *in regard to* or *with respect to* in front of the noun.

● **GOOF-PROOF SAMPLES** ●
AVOID USING –*WISE*

Businesswise, this year hasn't been as good as last year.
With respect to our business, this year has not been as good as last year.

We're in an excellent position this year, *resourcewise.*
With respect to our resources, we're in an excellent position this year.

RULE #29: Don't Sound Like a Robot

Let your personality show through your writing.

● **GOOF-PROOF IT!** ●

Business writing should sound professional, not stiff or dull. Your writing will be more interesting and easier to read if you let your personality show through. Avoid sounding like a robot by following these guidelines:

- Don't be afraid to use contractions in your e-mails, especially when writing to colleagues you are familiar with.
- Don't be short with your reader. A one- or two-word e-mail with no greeting or closing salutation may come off as curt. Always include a closing salutation and/or your first name at the end of an e-mail. Avoid signing off or addressing people with initials, and use friendly language, especially when you're delegating tasks or asking for favors.
- As a general rule, don't use words or phrases that would sound archaic or wooden if said out loud.
- Don't be afraid to use the occasional exclamation point, especially when thanking or complimenting someone.
- Always keep your own personality and individual preferences in mind. Never write anything that makes you feel uncomfortable.

> *Compare:*
> J: Leave the finished reports on my desk before you leave. I will look over them tonight and give you my comments in the morning.
>   K

> *With:*
> James,
> Please leave the finished reports on my desk before you leave today. I'll look them over tonight, and we can talk about any changes or revisions tomorrow morning.

Thanks for all your help!
   Karen

Compare:
The files you requested will be available presently. I will notify you once they have been properly converted and formatted. If you have any inquiries about the conversion or formatting process, please bring them to my attention. Thank you for your patience.

With:
Hank,
The files you asked for yesterday will take longer to convert and format than I originally thought. Thanks for being so patient. I'll let you know as soon as they're ready. If you have any questions, just let me know.
— Stephanie

RULE #30: Formality versus Informality

The level of formality you use in writing a specific letter, memo, e-mail, or report will depend on your audience and current accepted standards.

● **GOOF-PROOF IT!** ●

General guidelines for business writing today fall between the very formal (proper, stuffy, and distanced) and the very informal (use of slang, relaxed, and intimate). The level of formality should increase when your audience is of a higher rank, or is less familiar to you.

If you are writing to a colleague whom you know well, and with whom you frequently correspond, your level of formality may decrease. However, always retain the *business* in business writing. Avoid slang, possibly offensive language, and other examples of extreme informality.

● **GOOF-PROOF CHECKLIST** ●
FORMAL WRITING

✓ Avoid slang words and phrases.
✓ Use full words rather than contractions (*I will*, not *I'll*; *could have*, not *could've*).
✓ Refer to others with a title (Mr., Ms., CEO, Esquire).
✓ Use formal opening and closing salutations.
✓ Don't use five words when one will get the point across, or use words considered archaic or pretentious (*according to*, not *as per*; *determine*, not *ascertain*; *think about*, not *cogitate*).

[*QUIZ*]

Rate the following words as either formal (F) or informal (I). The answers can be found on page 174.

a. permit
b. allow

c. eliminate
d. get rid of

e. more
f. additional

g. cannot
h. unable to

i. help
j. assist

RULE #31: Avoid Colloquialisms

Informal and overused language do not belong in your workplace communications.

● GOOF-PROOF IT! ●

Colloquialisms are words and phrases appropriate for speech, and informal or casual writing. They don't belong in business writing unless you are trying to imitate speech or assume a very informal tone. They include contractions (*you'd, we'll, aren't, they're, shouldn't*), vulgarisms (obscene or offensive words), and clichés and slang (see below).

- **Contractions**
  The use of contractions is common in speech. In fact, speech can sound stilted if you avoid them. However, in business writing, contractions are usually too informal. They may be gaining acceptance in e-mails, but in letters, reports, and even most memos, they sound casual and unprofessional. Avoid using contractions in all but the least formal written business communications.

- **Clichés**
  Clichés should be avoided not only because they are informal, but also because they are overused. Your writing should project your own voice, without relying on stale phrases such as: *add insult to injury, cream of the crop, grin and bear it, pay the piper*, and *rat race*.

- **Slang**
  Slang is nonstandard English. Its significance is typically far-removed from either a word's denotative or connotative meaning, and is particular to certain groups (therefore, excluding some readers). Examples include: *blow off, canned, no sweat*, and *thumbs down (or up)*.

[*QUIZ*]

Rewrite the following sentences to eliminate any colloquial words or phrases. The answers can be found on page 175.

1. In conclusion, we believe you shouldn't choose our competitor's product because they just don't get the technology the way we do.
2. The accident last Tuesday was a bummer; we must install new floor mats to avoid another one in the future.
3. They're not sure if they'll attend the meeting that we're holding tomorrow.
4. If worse comes to worst, our firm could always tell the client their eleventh hour changes held up production.
5. The decision to cancel the trip has been made; you need to roll with the punches instead of crying over spilled milk.

RULE #32: Don't Bewilder Your Readers with Jargon

Workplace jargon and specialized language should be avoided or used sparingly.

• GOOF-PROOF IT! •

You won't get your message across efficiently if your reader has to consult a dictionary to understand what you have written. Write to your audience using language they will understand, eliminating or keeping to a minimum your use of business jargon.

- **Buzzwords**
  Buzzwords are real words, with real meanings, used in trendy ways for business purposes. This type of business slang is at best pompous, and at worst, confusing. And like other forms of slang, buzzwords don't belong in business writing.

  Examples include: *resultful* (gets results), *suboptimal* (not the best), *guesstimate* (estimate), *leverage* (use), *modality* (method), and *right-sizing* (cutting excess).

- **Technobabble**
  If you work in a field that constantly generates new words, or uses highly technical or field specific language, you and your colleagues will undoubtedly use those words in conversation with one another, and in writing for an audience of your peers. However, when corresponding with a client, or someone else connected with your business but not in the same field, it should not be used. Without writing down to your audience, explain yourself using words that may be understood by all.

• GOOF-PROOF SAMPLE •
TECHNOJARGON

GlobalCommand, LLC is pleased to announce a strategic partnership with the Wyckoff Group. Specifically, GlobalCommand, LLC will develop a secure global communications network designed to meet the Wyckoff Group's demand for bandwidth-rich services at significantly lower price points, plus improved quality of service.

GlobalCommand, LLC provides secure global communications through the following services:

- worldwide satellite connectivity
- Internet broadband access to remote locations
- voice over IP (VoIP)
- Virtual Private Networks (VPN)
- streaming video and video conferencing
- global data integration and networking

GlobalCommand, LLC's focus is on connecting organizations to remote locations where traditional, terrestrial-based networks do not reach and satellite is the optimum or only medium available to provide a high-speed, always-on connection. We are an efficient, reliable approach to global connectivity and security.

Capacity-Security-Global Reach—Redundancy Prevention:

These are the building blocks necessary to provide your business with superior, dependable communications. Through our services and solutions, any Internet provider, business customer, content provider, or telecommunications carrier can receive the benefits of fault-tolerant telecommunications through robust security products and communications services that operate seamlessly across time zones and national borders.

Did you identify these words and phrases as technojargon?

- *bandwidth-rich services*
- *terrestrial-based networks*
- *fault-tolerant telecommunications*

What words or phrases might you use in their place when communicating with a non-technical audience?

- Legalese
  Lawyers must also take care to avoid sounding pompous and confusing their audience. When writing to those who did not attend law school, avoid legal terms that are not commonly understood. Compare the first example with the second:

  > The following adjudication should be read in conjunction therewith the aforementioned financial reports.

  > This verdict should be read in conjunction with the financial reports.

● PUTTING IT ALL TOGETHER ●

When writing for a workplace audience, you must choose your words carefully. That means understanding their meanings, and being sensitive to their power. The wrong words not only make you seem less intelligent, but they can also confuse, annoy, or even offend your readers.

● GOOF-PROOF GUIDELINES ●

Choose words wisely by following the Goof-Proof guidelines:

- Learn the meanings of commonly confused words (those that sound or look similar, but have different meanings) and end the confusion in your writing.
- Learn the meanings of frequently misused words, and use them correctly.
- Don't use words considered non- or substandard English.
- Replace biased language with inclusive language to keep your writing from alienating or offending your audience.

- Understand the positive and negative connotations of the words you use. The wrong connotation can not only confuse, but also offend your readers.
- Avoid overusing the suffix *-wise.*
- Write in your own voice to avoid sounding like a robot.
- Use the level of formality appropriate to your reader(s).
- Keep colloquialisms, such as slang and clichés, out of your business writing.
- Don't use pompous or confusing jargon, such as legalese, technobabble, or buzzwords.

THE GOOF – UP: NOT UNDERSTANDING THE BASIC MECHANICS OF WRITING

No matter how great an idea you come up with, or how persuasively you can argue a point, an inability to express yourself clearly and accurately through the written word will hinder your success at work. The rules of mechanics are complex; in fact, they sometimes confuse even professional writers.

However, you do not need to become a strict grammarian in order to speak and write well. A few dozen grammar, spelling, punctuation, and capitalization mistakes account for the majority. If you learn these common errors and how to avoid or correct them, your writing will greatly improve. Therefore, the focus of this section is on those errors that occur most frequently.

The following rules will teach you the writing mechanics you need to know at work. Remember: Your business writing is a reflection of you. Your documents will show that you are smart, articulate, and dependable when you use proper spelling, punctuation, and grammar.

RULE #33: Remember the Parts of Speech

Identifying the six major parts of speech, and learning their most common usage errors, will help you write clear, concise sentences.

● GOOF-PROOF IT! ●

Some parts of speech are more difficult than others. The following are those you will encounter most frequently in business writing, with usage explanations and examples.

● Nouns

Nouns name people, places, things, and ideas. In a sentence, they are often the subject—the person, place, thing, or idea that is doing or being something. Nouns may be:

- proper (naming specific individual people, places, or things, such as *Susan B. Anthony, Santa Fe*, and *Kleenex*)
- abstract (naming ideas or qualities, such as *freedom* and *confusion*)
- collective (naming groups of people, animals, or things, such as *doctors, rabbits*, and *radios*)
- compound (formed by combining two or more words, such as *freelance, drive-in*, and *power of attorney*)

● Pronouns

Pronouns refer back to or take the place of nouns. They should:

- agree in number (a singular pronoun must be used for a singular noun)

  Correct: If *the student* passes this course, *she* will graduate.
  Incorrect: If *the student* passes this course, *they* will graduate.

- agree in person
  Don't switch back and forth in your writing from the first person (*I*) to the second (*you*) or third (*he, she, they, it*).
  First person pronouns: *I, me, we, us*
  Second: *you*
  Third: *he, she, him, her, they, them*

  Correct: When a *person* comes to class, *he* or *she* should have his homework ready.

  Incorrect: When a *person* comes to class, *you* should have your homework ready.

- be a specific reference to a noun
  It should be obvious to your reader which noun the pronoun refers to.

  Incorrect: Kim spends all his time reading and playing soccer, but it isn't good for him.

  What isn't good for him? Reading, playing soccer, or both?

  Correct: Kim spends all his time reading and playing soccer. Too much soccer isn't good for him; he should play some basketball, too.

  Incorrect: It's been years since *they* tore down that building.

  Who is they?

  Correct: It's been years since the demolition crew tore down that building.

  Incorrect: I went on the trip with Emily and Nancy, and we took her laptop.

  Whose laptop? Emily's or Nancy's

  Correct: I went on the trip with Emily and Nancy, and we took Nancy's laptop.

Verbs

Verbs depict action or a state of being. They tell the reader what is happening to the subject of a sentence. Although there are many types of verbs, the three you should be most aware of are *transitive, intransitive*, and *helping*.

Some verbs require an object to complete their meaning: *She gave* _____*?* Gave what? *She gave money to the church.* These verbs are called *transitive*. Verbs that are *intransitive* do not require objects: *The building collapsed.* In English, you cannot tell the difference between a transitive and intransitive verb by its form; you have to see how the verb is functioning within the sentence. In fact, a verb can be both transitive and intransitive: *The monster collapsed the building by sitting on it.* vs. *The monster collapsed.*

Helping verbs or auxiliary verbs such as *will, shall, may, might, can, could, must, ought to, should, would, used to,* and *need* are used in conjunction with main verbs to express shades of time and mood. The combination of helping verbs with main verbs creates what are called verb phrases or verb strings. In the following sentence, *will have been* are helping or auxiliary verbs and *studying* is the main verb; the whole verb string is italicized:

As of next August, I *will have been studying* chemistry for ten years.

• Adjectives

Adjectives describe or modify nouns or pronouns. They add information by describing people, places, or things in a sentence. These words add spice to our writing.

Adjectives can take the following forms:

- descriptive (qualify the properties or behavior of nouns or pronouns: *pretty, turquoise, heavy*)
  She loves *red* roses.
  The dog was *large* and *mean*.

- limiting (place boundaries or limits on the noun or pronoun they are modifying: *this, whose, any*)

  This hat isn't mine.

  I don't want *any* ketchup on my hamburger.
- compound (formed by combining two or more adjectives: *full-time, brown-eyed, long-haired*)

  He found a *full-time* job.

  The *long-haired* dog shed all over the carpet.
- articles (the words *the*, *a*, and *an*)

  The house is up for sale.

  Can you hand me *an* apple?

● Adverbs

Adverbs are words that describe verbs, clauses, adjectives, and other adverbs. They are easily spotted because most of them end in *–ly*, such as *slowly, quickly, abruptly*.

For example:

The black cat moved *slowly*.

The *ridiculously* long book was impossible to finish in one sitting.

When writing a question, you must use an interrogative adverb such as *how, what, where, when,* or *why*. These adverbs ask questions that modify verbs, clauses, adjectives, and other adverbs.

● GOOF-PROOF RULE OF THUMB ●

The word *good* is an adjective, not an adverb, and should be used to describe nouns. In the following sentence, *good* describes the noun *pasta:* The pasta you made last night was *good*. *Good* should never be used as an adverb. In the following sentence, *good* is used to describe the verb *played*, which is incorrect: I played *good* in the basketball game. The correct word to use in such instances is *well, good*'s adverb counterpart. Written correctly, the sentence would read, "I played *well* in the basketball game."

• Prepositions

Prepositions connect words that link a noun or pronoun to another word in a sentence. They are often used to show a relationship of space or time.

For example:

The <u>box</u> *on* your <u>desk</u> is your birthday present.
The <u>holiday</u> that follows immediately *after* your <u>birthday</u> is Valentine's Day.

The first sentence uses the preposition *on* to describe the spatial relationship between the *box* and the *desk*. The second sentence uses the preposition *after* to describe the time relationship between *holiday* and *birthday*. *On your desk* and *after your birthday* are prepositional phrases.

COMMON PREPOSITIONS							
aboard	about	above	after	among	around	at	before
behind	below	beneath	beside	between	by	except	for
from	in	inside	into	like	of	off	on
outside	over	to	under	up	upon	until	with
within							

The three most common problems with prepositions are:

1. Using Them Unnecessarily
    Because it is so important in business writing to get to the point concisely, unnecessary prepositions should be avoided. Remember that when two or more prepositions are used together, chances are at least one is unnecessary.

Poor form:	I cleaned *up under* the kitchen cabinets.
Good form:	I cleaned *under* the kitchen cabinets.
Poor form:	She likes all sports *except for* soccer.
Good form:	She likes all sports *except* soccer.
Poor form:	They looked *outside of* the house for the lost cat.
Good form:	They looked *outside* the house for the lost cat.

2. Using the Wrong One in a Standard Combination
Certain words must always be followed by certain prepositions. These necessary prepositions are always used in combination with their respective supported words. Below are two examples of required prepositions—the preposition is in italics and the supported word is underlined. It is important to remember that they must always be used together:

> You must <u>account</u> *for* every item on your expense report.
> The meal <u>consists</u> *of* eight separate courses.

Here is a list of several required prepositional pairings:

account for	agree upon	angry with	argue about
compare to	correspond with	differ from	different than
identical to	independent of	interested in	speak with

3. Confusing *Between* and *Among*
The third common mistake with prepositions involves the use of *between* and *among*. *Between* is used when talking about two things. *Among* is used when talking about more than two things:

> The boss had to decide *between* cutting new hires, or handing out Christmas bonuses.
> The work was divided evenly *among* marketing, finance, and operations.

• GOOF-PROOF RULE OF THUMB •

Of all the rules governing prepositions, none is more famous than: *Never end a sentence with a preposition!* While this rule holds true for many situations, it is not an absolute. You can still end a sentence with a preposition if it makes the sentence flow better. For example, in popular speech, it sounds much more natural to say "That's all I can think of" than "That's all of which I can think."

The best technique for deciding to keep or remove prepositions at the end of sentences is to use your ear. What would the statement sound like if you kept—or dropped—the preposition? What point are you trying to emphasize in your statement? Is this a formal statement or a casual conversational statement?

The timeless question of *to keep or to cut* the dangling preposition ultimately comes down to the desired effect. Here are some examples of prepositions placed in different positions within sentences:

> I thought I knew what company she worked *for.*
> I thought I knew *for which* company she worked.

The first sentence sounds like a casual conversation, although it does not strictly adhere to the rule of not ending a sentence with a preposition. But, it does sound natural. The second sentence follows the grammatical rule, but it is not the kind of statement you are likely to hear in everyday conversation. This sentence is more formal than the first, but may be appropriate in certain situations.

Many times, short questions are ended in prepositions. Here are some acceptable and unacceptable examples. Note that the unacceptable sentences could be improved simply by dropping the prepositions at the end.

Good Form:
> Does he have anything to worry *about?*
> What did you use to make it *with?*
> What is the report comprised *of?*

Poor Form:
> Is the construction project over *with?*
> Where is the report *at?*
> Where do you want to go *to?*

RULE #34: Avoid Dangling Participles and Misplaced Modifiers

As stated at the beginning of this section, a few types of errors account for most of the grammatical mistakes found in business writing. What follows are ways to avoid dangling participles and misplaced modifiers.

● GOOF-PROOF IT! ●

Dangling participles and misplaced modifiers, although some-times difficult to recognize, are easily fixed by rearranging the sentence.

A *dangling participle* is a phrase or clause, using a verb end-ing in *–ing* that does not refer to the subject of the sentence it modifies. Since it is so critical in business writing to make the reader understand your point easily and exactly, dangling modi-fiers (and indeed any ambiguous language) must be avoided.

Incorrect: While working on the annual financial report, Tony's com-puter crashed.

(Was the computer working on the report?)

Correct: While Tony was working on the annual financial report, his computer crashed.

Note that correcting a dangling participle involves adding and/or rearranging the words in a sentence to make the meaning clear.

Incorrect: While reading the morning paper, the noisy coffee pot dis-tracted Jim.
Correct: While Jim was reading the morning paper, he was dis-tracted by the noisy coffee pot.

Or

The noisy coffee pot distracted Jim while he was reading the morning paper.

A *misplaced modifier* is a word or phrase that describes something, but is in the wrong place in the sentence. It isn't dangling; no extra words are needed; the modifier is just in the wrong place. The danger of misplaced modifiers, as with dangling modifiers, is that they confuse meaning.

> *Incorrect:*　The assistant forwarded the e-mail to his boss covering the the new proposal.

Who or what is covering the new proposal? His boss or the e-mail? To say exactly what is meant, the modifying clause *covering the new proposal* should be moved to modify *e-mail*.

> *Correct:*　The assistant forwarded the e-mail covering the new proposal to his boss.

RULE #35: Noun/Verb Agreement

Nouns and verbs must agree in number. A singular noun takes a singular verb, and a plural noun takes a plural verb.

● **GOOF-PROOF IT!** ●

To achieve subject-verb agreement, first determine whether your subject is singular or plural, and then pair it with the correct verb form.

Incorrect:	Tim and Fran *is* a great couple.
	One of her boys *are* going to school.
Correct:	Tim and Fran *are* a great couple. (Plural subject takes plural verb)
	One of her boys *is* going to school. (Singular subject takes singular verb)

Agreement may be difficult to determine when the noun follows the verb. Common examples include sentences that begin with *there is* and *there are*, and *here is* and *here are*. When editing your work, remember to first determine whether your subject is singular or plural, and them match it to the correct verb.

Incorrect:	There's too many meetings scheduled on Tuesday morning.
Correct:	There *are* too many meetings scheduled on Tuesday morning.
Incorrect:	Here's the memos you asked me to write.
Correct:	Here *are* the memos you asked me to write.

● **GOOF-PROOF CHECKLIST** ●

The more complex the sentence, the more difficult it is to determine noun/verb agreement. Here are some guidelines that may help you:

✓ If a compound, singular subject is connected by *and*, the verb must be plural. (Both the 10-speed *and* the hybrid *are* appropriate for the bike race.)

✓ If a compound, singular subject is connected by *or* or *nor*, the verb must be singular. (Neither the 10-speed *nor* the hybrid *is* appropriate for a trail race, however.)

✓ If one plural and one singular subject are connected by *or* or *nor*, the verb agrees with the closest subject. (Neither a fast bike *nor perfect trails are* going to help you win if you do not train.)

QUIZ

Correct the following sentences, if necessary. The answers can be found on page 175.

1. Shelly and her husband is traveling to Spain.
2. Neither of your newsletter items were clearly written.
3. Both of the managers is rumored to be fired after losing the account.
4. One of the pitchers injured his elbow.
5. Either you or your brother are going to have to talk to your parents.

RULE #36: Active versus Passive Voice

Strive to write in the active, rather than passive, voice. Not only is it more clear and more direct, but the active voice conveys your meaning more easily.

● GOOF-PROOF IT! ●

If you use the passive voice, your sentences may become too wordy, or lack focus. The last thing you want in business writing is long sentences that are confusing to the reader. The good news is, passive-voice errors are easy to omit from your writing.

When you write in the active voice, the subject of the sentence causes, or is the source of, the action. In the passive voice, the subject is acted upon. Compare:

Active:	The gentleman asked for another glass of wine.
Passive:	Another glass of wine was asked for by the gentleman.
Active:	I misplaced my wallet.
Passive:	My wallet was misplaced by me.
Active:	The human resources team has selected three finalists for the open position.
Passive:	Three finalists for the open position have been selected by the human resources team.

Note the simplicity and directness of the first sentence in each pair. The second sentences, written in the passive voice, are clunky and noticeably longer.

There are situations in which the passive voice is acceptable, or even desired. Scientific writing, for example, needs to focus on data, and not the person who is presenting the data. Since the passive voice tends to put the subject in the background, it is perfect for this type of writing.

• GOOF-PROOF RULE OF THUMB •

The passive voice is especially out of place in business writing because it can lead to sentences that don't have a clear subject. Sometimes politicians or shifty corporate officers intentionally employ the passive voice in order to avoid taking the blame for something. How many times have you heard, "Mistakes were made," or "It is regrettable that . . . ?" The passive voice allows the speaker to apologize without really apologizing.

If you find yourself in a situation in the workplace where you must apologize, use the active voice. Instead of "I regret that the client didn't like the presentation," say "I'm sorry the client didn't like my presentation." Taking ownership of a problem or a mistake is not pleasant, but it adds to your integrity and positive image at work.

RULE #37: Sentence Fragments and Run-on Sentences

A sentence fragment is a group of words that do not express a complete thought. Run-on sentences are made up of two or more independent clauses or complete sentences placed together into one sentence without proper punctuation.

● GOOF-PROOF IT! ●

Sentence fragments are often missing a subject or verb, and may be dependent clauses. Fragments also can be phrases or parts of other sentences. There are two basic ways to correct sentence fragments:

1. Add a subject.
2. Add an independent clause.

● GOOF-PROOF SAMPLES ●
SENTENCE FRAGMENTS

Fragment:	At the zoo.
Sentence:	*We had fun* at the zoo.
Fragment:	Cried a lot.
Sentence:	*She* cried a lot.
Fragment:	Can't go to the store.
Sentence:	*He* can't go to the store.
Fragment:	When we finished the game.
Sentence:	When we finished the game, *we went home.*

There are many structure mistakes that result in run-on sentences, so there are no hard and fast rules. However, proper punctuation and careful adherence to grammar rules should prevent you from making this type of goof-up.

Here are some strategies for correcting run-on sentences.

1. Break up the run-on sentence into two or more complete sentences.
2. Use a comma and a conjunction (*and, or, nor, for, so, but, yet*) to set apart an independent clause.
3. Break up the sentence by inserting a semicolon between two clauses.
4. Use a dash to separate parts of the sentence.
5. Add a dependent clause (use words such as *because, after, since,* and *while*).

● GOOF-PROOF SAMPLES ● RUN-ON SENTENCES

Run-on: We were hungry and John was tired so we had to stop at the first rest area that we saw.

Sentence: *Since* we were hungry and John was tried, we had to stop at the first rest area that we saw.

Run-on: Kim studied hard for the test that's why he got an 'A'.

Sentence: Kim studied hard for the test, *and* that's why he got an 'A'.

Run-on: Patty took flying lessons every Saturday so she couldn't go to the picnic and she couldn't go to the graduation party either but she has already signed up for another group of flying lessons because she likes it so much.

Sentence: *Because* Patty took flying lessons every Saturday, she couldn't go to the picnic or the graduation party; she has already signed up for another group of flying lessons, though, because she likes them so much.

RULE #38: Verb Tense Shifts

Verb tenses must be consistent within each sentence and paragraph.

● **GOOF-PROOF IT!** ●

Unnecessary shifts from one tense to another not only sound unprofessional, but may obscure meaning as well. For instance, when describing an event in the past, all verbs should be in the past tense.

● **GOOF-PROOF SAMPLES** ●
VERB TENSE SHIFTS

Incorrect: When we finished our lunch, we *decide* to take a walk.

Correct: When we finished our lunch, we *decided* to take a walk.

Incorrect: Last year, the governor said he *is campaigning* for our candidate.

Correct: Last year, the governor said he *would campaign* for our candidate, or Last year the governor said he *was campaigning* for our candidate.

RULE #39: Double Negatives

As with verb tense shifts, the use of two negatives (such as "I won't never give up") in a sentence not only sounds incompetent, but it can also obscure meaning.

• GOOF-PROOF IT! •

The use of double negatives is unnecessary and redundant. Eliminate them from your writing.

• GOOF-PROOF RULE OF THUMB • NEGATIVES

There are more negatives than just the obvious *no, not, never, neither*, and *nor*. Remember that *hardly* and *barely* are negatives, too. If you are using those words, you have a negative, so you do not need to double up.

• GOOF-PROOF SAMPLES • NEGATIVES

Incorrect:	We hardly never see movies.
Correct:	We hardly *ever* see movies.
Incorrect:	There aren't no tickets left.
Correct:	There aren't *any* tickets left.
Incorrect:	Mary doesn't like neither of those books.
Correct:	Mary doesn't like *either* of those books.
Incorrect:	Vegans don't eat dairy products nor meat.
Correct:	Vegans don't eat dairy products *or* meat.

[*QUIZ*]

Circle only the sentences that are correct. The answers can be found on page 175.

1. We barely didn't catch the train.
2. Lee didn't have nothing to say at the meeting.
3. Don't give up on your puppy; he just needs more training.
4. Heather never went nowhere on vacation.
5. I didn't know which book to consult.

RULE #40: Don't Make Spelling Mistakes

Spelling mistakes and the business world do not mix. Strive to improve your spelling skills, always use the spelling tools at your fingertips, and never knowingly send out a document with a typo.

● GOOF-PROOF IT! ●

Spelling errors in business writing are embarrassing, and can make you seem unprofessional. They can also be costly. Menus, brochures, and advertising campaigns with misspellings are expensive wastes of money.

On a smaller scale, the repeated misspelling of simple words in your e-mails, memos, letters, or reports take away from the seriousness of your writing. Spelling errors can make you appear careless, lazy, and unintelligent. Learn and use the following rules, and your spelling will improve.

Putting in a little time will improve your spelling quickly. You can learn simple spelling rules that cover the few dozen mistakes that account for the majority of errors. In addition, you can become a more proficient user of your computer's spell check feature.

- Basic Spelling Rules: I Before E

  I before E except after C, or when sounding like A (as in neighbor or weigh).

  Though it has a few exceptions, this simple rule is worth remembering. The majority of the time, it works.

  Some examples of the exceptions:

  After C: *ceiling, conceive, deceive, perceive, receipt, receive, deceit, conceit*

  When sounding like A: *neighbor, freight, beige, sleigh, weight, vein, weigh*

  Others: *either, neither, feint, foreign, forfeit, height, leisure, weird, seize,* and *seizure*

- Basic Spelling Rules: Doubling Final Consonants

  When adding an ending to a word that ends in a consonant, you double the consonant if:

➤ the ending begins with a vowel (such as *–ing, –ed, –age, –er, –ence, –ance,* and *–al*)

➤ the last syllable of the word is accented and that syllable ends in an single vowel followed by a single consonant (words with only one syllable are always accented). *Stop* becomes *stopping, stopped, stoppage,* or *stopper* because *stop* has only one syllable (so it is accented), and it ends in a single consonant preceded by a single vowel.

Here are some other examples of words that meet the doubling requirements:

run: running, runner
slam: slamming, slammed
nag: nagged, nagging
incur: incurred, incurring
kid: kidding, kidder
plan: planned, planning, planner
begin: beginning, beginner
set: setting
transmit: transmitting, transmittal, transmitted

• Basic Spelling Rules: Dropping Final E's and Y's

When adding an ending to a word that ends with a silent *e*, drop the final *e* if the ending begins with a vowel, such as *advancing* and *surprising*.

If the ending begins with a consonant, keep the final *e*, as in *advancement* and *likeness*.

However, if the silent *e* is preceded by another vowel, drop the *e* when adding any ending: *argument, argued, truly.*)

● GOOF-PROOF RULE OF THUMB ●

● Exceptions to the Rules

To avoid confusion and mispronunciation, the final *e* is kept in words such as *mileage* and words where the final *e* is preceded by a soft *g* or *c: changeable, courageous, manageable, management, noticeable*. The word *management*, for example, would be pronounced with a hard *g* sound if not for the *e* after the *g*. If the root word ends with a silent *e*, and the suffix begins with a vowel, then take off the silent *e* and add the suffix.

come + ing = coming

If the root word ends with a consonant followed by the letter *y*, change the *y* to *i* and add the suffix.

reply + ed = replied

- Basic Spelling Rules: Plurals
  Most words are made plural by simply adding an *s*. However, if a word ends in *x* or *s*, -*sh* or -*ch*, the suffix -*es* must be added to form a plural.

  church/churches
  box/boxes
  plus/plusses

If the word ends in a consonant plus -*y*, change the -*y* into -*ie* and add an -*s* to form the plural.

enemy/enemies
baby/babies

When in doubt, look up the singular form in the dictionary, where you will also find the plural listed.

• GOOF-PROOF LIST •
COMMONLY MISSPELLED WORDS

1.	absence	37.	descend
2.	abundance	38.	desperate
3.	accidentally	39.	development
4.	accommodate	40.	dilemma
5.	acknowledgment	41.	discrepancy
6.	acquaintance	42.	eighth
7.	aggravate	43.	eligible
8.	alibi	44.	embarrass
9.	alleged	45.	equivalent
10.	ambiguous	46.	euphoria
11.	analysis	47.	existence
12.	annual	48.	exuberance
13.	argument	49.	feasible
14.	awkward	50.	February
15.	basically	51.	fifth
16.	boundary	52.	forcibly
17.	bulletin	53.	forfeit
18.	calendar	54.	formerly
19.	canceled	55.	fourth
20.	cannot	56.	fulfill
21.	cemetery	57.	grateful
22.	coincidence	58.	grievance
23.	collectible	59.	guarantee
24.	committee	60.	guidance
25.	comparative	61.	harass
26.	completely	62.	hindrance
27.	condemn	63.	ideally
28.	congratulations	64.	implement
29.	conscientious	65.	independence
30.	consistent	66.	indispensable
31.	convenient	67.	inoculate
32.	correspondence	68.	insufficient
33.	deceive	69.	interference
34.	definitely	70.	interrupt
35.	dependent	71.	jealousy
36.	depot	72.	jewelry

73. judgment
74. leisure
75. length
76. lenient
77. liaison
78. lieutenant
79. lightning
80. loophole
81. losing
82. maintenance
83. maneuver
84. mathematics
85. millennium
86. minuscule
87. miscellaneous
88. misspell
89. negotiable
90. ninth
91. occasionally
92. occurred
93. omission
94. opportunity
95. outrageous
96. pamphlet
97. parallel
98. perceive
99. permanent
100. perseverance
101. personnel
102. possess
103. potato
104. precede
105. preferred
106. prejudice
107. prevalent
108. privilege
109. procedure
110. proceed
111. prominent
112. pronunciation
113. quandary
114. questionnaire
115. receipt
116. receive
117. recommend
118. reference
119. referred
120. regardless
121. relevant
122. religious
123. remembrance
124. reservoir
125. responsible
126. restaurant
127. rhythm
128. ridiculous
129. roommate
130. scary
131. scissors
132. secretary
133. separate
134. souvenir
135. specifically
136. sufficient
137. supersede
138. temperament
139. temperature
140. truly
141. twelfth
142. ubiquitous
143. unanimous
144. usually
145. usurp
146. vacuum
147. vengeance
148. visible
149. Wednesday
150. wherever

QUIZ

Can you spot the errors? Determine whether the following words are correct or incorrect by circling the appropriate term. The answers can be found on page 176.

1. abundence	correct	incorrect
2. basically	correct	incorrect
3. collectable	correct	incorrect
4. existance	correct	incorrect
5. fullfill	correct	incorrect
6. globaly	correct	incorrect
7. harrass	correct	incorrect
8. lightning	correct	incorrect
9. misspell	correct	incorrect
10. ocassionally	correct	incorrect
11. paralell	correct	incorrect
12. possess	correct	incorrect
13. questionnare	correct	incorrect
14. receipt	correct	incorrect
15. relavant	correct	incorrect
16. scarey	correct	incorrect
17. separate	correct	incorrect
18. temperture	correct	incorrect
19. vaccum	correct	incorrect
20. whereever	correct	incorrect

• Using Computer Spell Checkers

There is no excuse for not using spell check. It's fast and simple, and catches many common spelling errors and typos. However, spell check is not fool-proof. You should be aware of its two most important limitations, and rely on other methods to catch possible errors, especially for more important documents.

• Non-Word versus Real-Word Errors

Most of us think of spelling errors in the first category, that is, a string of letters that does not make a real word. You might type *sevn* instead of *seven*, or *th* for *the*. Spell check is an excellent tool for catching these types of mistakes. However, if a report you are writing includes information about the seven layers of management in your company, and you leave off the *s* and type *even*, spell check won't flag your error.

This is known as a real-word error. You have typed a legitimate, correctly spelled word; it's just not the word you meant to type, and it doesn't convey the meaning you intended. Spell check can't find these types of errors.

• Proper Nouns

Spell check uses a dictionary that does not include most proper nouns and words in other categories, such as the names of chemicals. You can always add a word or words to the dictionary once you are sure of its spelling, but the first time, you will need to use another source (a reliable print one is best) to verify the spelling.

• Professional Proofreading Tricks to Catch Spelling Errors

A few professional proofreading tricks can help you catch what spell check can't.

1. *Take your time.* Studies show that waiting at least twenty minutes before proofreading your work can increase your likelihood of finding errors. Get up from your computer, take a break or move on to some other task, and then come back to your writing.
2. *Read backward.* Go through your writing from the last word to the first, focusing on each individual word, rather than on the context.

3. *Ask for help*. A pair of fresh eyes may find mistakes that you have overlooked dozens of times, and one or more of your colleagues may be better at finding spelling and grammar errors than you are.

4. *Go under cover*. Print out a draft copy of your writing, and read it with a blank piece of paper over it, revealing just one sentence at a time. This technique will encourage a careful line-by-line edit.

5. *Watch the speed limit*. No matter which proofreading technique(s) you use, slow down. Reading at your normal speed won't give you enough time to spot errors.

6. *Know yourself*. Keep track of the kinds of errors you typically make. Common spelling errors can be caught by spell check if you add the word or words to the spell check dictionary. When you know what you are looking for, you are more likely to find it.

RULE #41: Use Punctuation Marks Correctly

Punctuation allows you to convey certain tones and inflections, give emphasis where needed, and separate longer sentences into more easily defined and understood segments.

• GOOF-PROOF IT! •

There are dozens of different punctuation marks in the English language; those covered in this section are often used in business today, and present the most challenges to their users. Remember, if you punctuate effectively, your writing will not only communicate your message, but will also do so clearly and with personality—the desired effect of most business writing.

• The Apostrophe

Apostrophes are used to indicate ownership. Eight rules cover all of the situations in which they may appear.

1. Add *'s* to form the singular possessive, even when the noun ends in *s:*

    The *school's* lunchroom needs to be cleaned.
    The *drummer's* solo received a standing ovation.
    Mr. Perkins's persuasive essay was very convincing.

2. A few plurals, not ending in *s*, also form the possessive by adding *'s:*

    The *children's* toys were found in every room of the house.
    The line for the *women's* restroom was too long.
    Men's shirts come in a variety of neck sizes.

3. Possessive plural nouns already ending in *s* need only the apostrophe added:

    The *customers'* access codes are confidential.
    The *students'* grades improved each semester.
    The flight *attendants'* uniforms were blue and white.

4. Indefinite pronouns show ownership by the addition of *'s*:

    Everyone's hearts were in the right place.

    Somebody's dog was barking all night.

    It was *no one's* fault that we lost the game.

5. Possessive pronouns never have apostrophes, even though some may end in *s:*

    Our car is up for sale.

    Your garden is beautiful.

    His handwriting is difficult to read.

6. Use an *'s* to form the plurals of letters, figures, and numbers used as words, as well as certain expressions of time and money. The expressions of time and money do not indicate ownership in the usual sense:

    She has a hard time pronouncing *s's*.

    My street address contains three *5's*.

    He packed a *week's* worth of clothing.

    The project was the result of a *year's* worth of work.

7. Show possession in the last word when using names of organizations and businesses, in hyphenated words, and in joint ownership:

    Sam and Janet's wedding was three month's ago.

    I went to visit my *great-grandfather's* alma mater.

    The Future Farmers of America's meeting was moved to Monday.

8. Apostrophes form contractions by taking the place of the missing letter or number. Do not use contractions in highly formal written presentations:

Poor form:	*We're* going out of town next week.
Good form:	*We are* going out of town next week.
Poor form:	*She's* going to write the next proposal.
Good form:	*She is* going to write the next proposal.
Poor form:	My supervisor was in the class of *'89.*
Good form:	My supervisor was in the class of *1989.*

• GOOF-PROOF RULE OF THUMB •
ITS VERSUS IT'S

Unlike most possessives, *its* does not contain an apostrophe. The word *it's* is instead a contraction of the words *it is*. The second *i* is removed, and replaced by an apostrophe.

When revising your writing, say the words *it is* when you come across *it's* or *its*. If they make sense, you should be using the contraction. If they don't, you need the possessive form, *its*, without an apostrophe.

| QUIZ |

Fill in the blanks with *its* or *it's* to complete the following sentences correctly. The answers can be found on page 176.

1. When _____ nice outside, Jorge enjoys hiking and camping.
2. Many people believe the big gas-guzzling car has seen _____ popularity dwindle.
3. _____ good form to send a thank you note after receiving a gift.
4. Store garlic in _____ own aerated container.
5. Janice feels _____ time to call another meeting.

• The Comma

The uses of commas are many, but seven rules provide the basics for their successful management in business writing. Many times their use is optional; if you are in doubt, as the saying goes, leave it out. Correct usage of commas is not as critical to the meaning of your sentences as it is with other punctuation marks. However, you should be aware of and practice proper use of them.

• GOOF-PROOF LIST •
THE FIVE PRIMARY USES OF COMMAS

1. Before *and, but, for, or, nor, yet, still,* when joining independent clauses.
2. Between all terms in a series, including the last two.
3. To set off parenthetical openers and afterthoughts.
4. Before and after parenthetical insertions.
5. In dates, titles, and quotations.

• Using Commas

1. Use commas to separate two sentences joined by a coordinating conjunction:

   Sophia went to the movies, *and* her brother went to a concert.

   Milton likes to read the newspaper, *but* he doesn't like to read magazines.

   We can leave together tomorrow afternoon, *or* we can leave separately tomorrow evening.

2. Use commas to separate words and word groups in a series of three or more:

   Carla, Lewis, and Stephanie met with the director for an audition.

   The dancers must *practice their routines, avoid junk food, and always be on time to class.*

   He performed a *fast, upbeat, and well-written* song.

3. Use commas to separate two adjectives when the word *and* could be inserted between them:

   Correct: He is a *knowledgeable, worthy* opponent.

   Incorrect: The *new, paperback* book was a joy to read.

   (You would not say, *new and paperback* book.)

• GOOF-PROOF RULE OF THUMB •
COMMA SPLICES

A comma splice is the incorrect use of a comma to connect two complete sentences. It creates a *run-on sentence* (see page 89). To correct a comma splice, you can:

- replace the comma with a period, forming two sentences.
- replace the comma with a semicolon.
- join the two clauses with a conjunction such as *and, because*, or *so*.

Comma splice: Our company received an award, we were number one in sales.

Corrected sentence: Our company received an award. We were number one in sales.
Our company received an award; we were number one in sales.
Our company received an award because we were number one in sales.

4. Use commas to set off words that are not part of the main structure of the sentence, such as introductory elements and expressions, or parenthetical clauses, that interrupt the flow of the sentence:
   For several months, we backpacked across Europe.
   When leaving the house, you should always make sure the doors are locked.
   No, I don't like spinach.

5. Use commas to set apart someone or something that has been insufficiently identified:
   Doug, *my best friend*, is coming for a visit.
   Janine, *who doesn't like chocolate*, declined a brownie.
   A picture of my dog, *Coral*, is on my desk at work.

6. Use a comma to separate the city from the state and after the state. This rule is currently being modified in some businesses to exclude the use of the second comma:

   Why did they send our product to *Trenton, New Jersey?*

   San Antonio, Texas is famous for its mild winters.

7. Use commas to surround degrees or titles used with names:

   Sally Crawford, *Ph.D,* lectures at schools around the country.

   Richard Bernard, *President of Sales,* is an asset to this company.

• The Serial Comma

A serial comma is used last in a list of items, after the word *and.* For instance, in the following example, the comma after *apples* is the serial comma:

At the store, I bought bananas, apples, and oranges.

The lack of a serial comma can cause confusion. In the sentence, *Cindy, Ann, and Sally were hired to file our documents,* the message is straightforward. But if the serial comma is dropped, it could be understood as Cindy being told that Ann and Sally were hired.

Cindy, Ann and Sally were hired to file our documents.

While its use has been debated for centuries, the serial comma clarifies the meaning of sentences. Since one of the main goals of business writing is the successful, accurate conveyance of information, the serial comma should be used whenever writing a list.

• **The Colon**

Colons appear at the end of a clause and can introduce:

- a list when the clause before the colon can stand as a complete sentence on its own.

  Correct: He signed up for four classes: geometry, physics, American literature, and religion.

  Incorrect: The classes he signed up for include: geometry, physics, American literature, and religion.

- a restatement or elaboration of the previous clause.

  Correct: Shari is a talented hairdresser: She attends a seminar each month and has been a professional for over 20 years.

  My boss wasn't able to attend the meeting: He had to fly to Houston this morning.

  Incorrect: Shari is a talented hairdresser: She is also the mother of two children.

  My boss wasn't able to attend the meeting: He graduated Summa Cum Laude.

• **The Semicolon**

Semicolons may be used in two ways: to separate independent clauses, and to separate the items in a list when those items contain commas.

- Use semicolons to separate independent clauses

  Case: Use a semicolon to separate independent clauses joined without a conjunction.

  Example: Four people worked on the project; only one received credit for it.

  Case: Use a semicolon to separate independent clauses that contain commas, even if the clauses are joined by a conjunction.

Example: The strays were malnourished, dirty, and ill; but Liz had a weakness for kittens, so she adopted them all.

Case: Use a semicolon to separate independent clauses that are connected with a conjunctive adverb that expresses a relationship between clauses.

Example: Victoria was insubordinate; therefore, she was fired.

- Use semicolons to separate items in a series that contain commas

    Case: Use a semicolon to show which sets of items go together.

    Example: The dates for our meetings are Monday, January 10; Tuesday, April 14; Monday, July 7; and Tuesday, October 11. She has lived in Omaha, Nebraska; Nutley, New Jersey; Amherst, Massachusetts; and Pensacola, Florida.

RULE #42: Don't Overuse Capital Letters

Capitalization is necessary both for specific words and to start sen-
tences and quotes. However, many writers overuse it, and, thus,
appear overly casual. Obey the rules of capitalization to ensure
that your writing maintains a professional look and tone.

● GOOF-PROOF IT! ●

Here are the six occasions that require capitalization:

- the first word of a sentence
- proper nouns (names of people, places, and things)
- the first word of a complete quotation, but not a partial quotation
- the first, last, and any other important words of a title
- languages
- the pronoun *I*, and any contractions made with it

● GOOF-PROOF RULE OF THUMB ●

Proper nouns require capitalization. Common nouns do not. How
can you tell the difference? A proper noun is specific, referring to
a specific person (*Juanita*), place (*England*), or thing (*Nissan*
Xterra). A common noun is general, referring to a general group
of people (*girl*), place (*country*), or thing (*vehicle*).

[*QUIZ*]

Correct any capitalization errors in the following sentences. The answers can be found on page 176.

1. We are going to Portugal on vacation this summer.
2. Next wednesday is dr. lee's lecture.
3. Do you want me to pick up the copies at the xerox machine?
4. Kevin is learning Chinese in school this year.
5. Make a right on Maple st., and then stop in front of the post office.

● PUTTING IT ALL TOGETHER ●

No matter how great an idea you come up with, or how persuasively you can argue a point, an inability to express yourself clearly and accurately through the written word will hinder your success at work. Your documents must show that you are smart, accurate, and dependable by using proper spelling, punctuation, and grammar.

● GOOF-PROOF GUIDELINES ●

- Be able to identify and correctly use the parts of speech.
- Nouns and verbs must agree in number. A singular noun takes a singular verb, and a plural noun takes a plural verb. Determine first whether your subject is singular or plural, and then pair it with the correct verb.
- Your use of verbs must be consistent. When describing an event in the past, all verbs should be in the past tense. Unnecessary shifts from one tense to another not only sound unprofessional, but may obscure meaning as well.
- Know the most common grammatical errors and how to avoid them.

- A dangling participle is a phrase or clause, using a verb ending in–*ing*, that says something different from what is intended because words are left out. Since it is so critical in business writing to make the reader understand your point easily and exactly, dangling participles must be avoided.

- A misplaced modifier is a word or phrase that describes something, but is in the wrong place in the sentence. It isn't dangling; no extra words are needed; the modifier is just in the wrong place. The danger of misplaced modifiers, as with dangling modifiers, is that they confuse meaning.

- Strive to write in the active rather than passive voice. Not only is it more clear and direct, but the active voice conveys your meaning more easily. If you use the passive voice, your sentences may become too wordy, and lack focus. The last thing you want in business writing is long sentences that are confusing to the reader.

- A sentence fragment is a group of words that, although punctuated as a sentence, does not express a complete thought. Fragments are often missing a subject or verb, and may be a dependent clause. Fragments also can be phrases or parts of other sentences.

- A run-on sentence is made up of two or more independent clauses or complete sentences placed together into one sentence without proper punctuation.

- The use of two negatives in a sentence not only sounds incompetent, but it can obscure meaning too.

- Spelling errors in business writing are embarrassing, and can make you seem unprofessional. Learn the Goof-Proof spelling rules and professional proofreading tricks to write error-free documents.

- Punctuation allows you to convey certain tones and inflections, give emphasis where needed, and separate longer sentences into more easily defined and understood segments. If you punctuate effectively, your writing will not only communicate your message, but do so clearly and with personality—the desired effect of most business writing.

THE GOOF – UP: CONFUSING THE TYPES OF BUSINESS WRITING

For your instruction and reference, rules for eight of the most common business writing formats are included in this section. You will read about each type and learn how to adapt the information to suit your business communication needs.

- e-mails
- basic business letters
- memos
- agendas
- proposals
- reports
- thank you letters
- instructions/directions

Keep in mind that your company may offer specific document templates that you are expected to use. If this is the case, do not substitute these formats. Instead, read the rules strictly for the concepts behind the formats and styles shown, and apply the concepts when using your company's templates.

Likewise, many word processing programs, such as Microsoft Word, offer document templates for you to use. You may incorporate the rules presented in this segment when you use the prefabricated templates provided by your word processing system.

RULE #43: Get E-mails in Order

Learning how to correctly write and format e-mails will allow you to enjoy their advantages while avoiding common (and often embarrassing) mistakes.

● GOOF-PROOF IT! ●

The use of e-mail in business settings has grown from a trend to standard practice. This cross between a telephone conversation and a memo has great advantages: It is faster to deliver than a memo, yet slower than a phone call. Following the guidelines below will help you craft Goof-Proof e-mails in no time.

● E-mail Formatting Guidelines

- Make your subject line compelling and clear. Describe the content of the e-mail in as few words as possible.
- Be brief. One screen length should be the limit for most e-mails. Longer messages sent electronically should be delivered as attachments.
- Check for grammar, spelling, and punctuation errors.
- Avoid logos and graphics, which take up too much computer space. Instead, use different fonts, dark and neutral colors, or different type sizes for emphasis.
- CC only those who need to read your e-mail.
- Use universal keywords and acronyms if it is common practice in your company.

- Break up information in longer e-mails by beginning with a summary (or table of contents), and using headings and sub-headings within the text.
- Strive for brevity when sending an attachment electronically. Do not repeat the substance of the attachment in the body of the e-mail.
- Don't use Emoticons; reserve smiley faces and winks for personal correspondence.
- Remember that formatting (such as the use of boldface, italics, underlining, graphics, and colors) often does not translate across servers. If you want to emphasize a heading or title, use all caps—but do so sparingly. All caps tend to come across to the reader as "shouting."
- Use the subject line wisely. Remember, other employees can read the subject lines of their co-workers' e-mails as they pass by their cubicles, so exercise decorum. Also, there is no excuse for omitting a subject title. A missing title is not mysterious or cool; it's unprofessional.

• GOOF-PROOF CHECKLIST •
POTENTIAL PROBLEMS

✓ Your reader will not hear your tone of voice, and may misinterpret your meaning if your words are not chosen carefully with their connotation in mind. For instance, the following sentences all convey a similar message, but will be interpreted very differently by the reader:

1. Tom, your report was a joke.
2. Tom, your report was TERRIBLE.
3. Tom, your report was unsatisfactory.
4. Tom, your report did not meet my expectations.
5. Tom, your report needs improvement.

✓ E-mails feel informal, so it may take some effort to remain businesslike.

✓ The size of a computer screen limits how much text the reader can see at one time. If you need to write something longer than a screen length, your subject might be better handled in a letter or memo.

● GOOF-PROOF SAMPLES ●
E-MAILS

1. *Straightforward business e-mail*—letter- or memo-like in tone and formality.

   Uses paragraph format, does not use contractions or small talk, only the business-related message included.

   Subject: Summer Schedule
   Date: Monday, May 22, 2003 09:48:02
   From: Jane Borowski jborowski@toolbox.com
   To: Annie Sloan asloan@toolbox.com

   Annie,
   Can we meet to review the summer schedule? I am available every day this week after 11:00.
   Please let me know which day and time is good for you.
   Thanks,
   Jane

2. *Less formal business e-mail*

   Includes small talk, contractions (*I'm, you're*), and an exclamation point, which come across as more friendly and casual (without being overly so).

   Subject: Summer Schedule
   Date: Monday, May 22, 2003 09:48:02
   From: Jane Borowski jborowski@toolbox.com
   To: Annie Sloan asloan@toolbox.com

Hi Annie. How was your vacation? I hope you had a wonderful time.
Now that you're back, can we meet to review the summer schedule?
I'm available every day this week after 11:00.

Please let me know which day and time is good for you.
Thanks!
Jane

3. *E-mail with attachment*
   When sending an attachment along with your e-mail,
   make specific reference to it in the body of the message
   so that the attachment is not overlooked by the recipient.

   Subject: Summer Schedule
   Date: Monday, May 25, 2003 09:48:02
   From: Jane Borowski jborowski@toolbox.com
   To: Annie Sloan asloan@toolbox.com

   Attached is the final version of the summer schedule. Please note all
   changes.

   Thanks,
   Jane

RULE #44: Perfect Your Business Letters

Business letters are not the place for guesswork or sloppy form. Learn the Goof-Proof way to format your letters to achieve the highest possible professional standard.

● GOOF-PROOF IT! ●

Business letters are typically written to people outside your company, and usually involve important information that will be referred to or referenced later.

Letters follow a certain format for three reasons:

1. To provide readers with certain necessary information (who wrote to whom, when, and about what).
2. To help organize information neatly.
3. To be reader-friendly; an established format means readers automatically know where to look to find certain information.

● Parts of a Business Letter

There can be up to 16 key parts of a letter, including the letterhead. Although you probably won't use all of them in every letter you write, their correct placement is essential in making your document look professional:

- *letterhead:* company stationery; used only for the first page of the letter
- *date:* the date on which the letter was written; placed at the top of the page, at least two lines below the letterhead symbol
- *inside address:* reader's name (or professional title) and address; should be flush left, at least two lines below the date
- *attention line:* used when your letter is addressed to a company, but you want someone specific to handle it; should be flush left in the inside address, either above the inside address, or immediately following the company's name

- *salutation:* a personal greeting to your reader; the salutation should be flush left, and placed two lines below the inside address
- *subject line:* consists of a few words that briefly describe the content of your letter; placed flush left, at least two lines below the salutation
- *body:* the actual message of your letter; begins two lines below the salutation, or subject line. Paragraphs are flush left or indented (depending on format); use single-spacing
- *closing:* ends the letter (typically: *Sincerely, Respectfully,* or *Best Regards*)
- *signature (company & signer) line:* name and job title of the person writing the letter; only used when writing on behalf of the company. The signature should appear four lines below the closing
- *reference initials:* references anyone (by initials) involved in the preparation of the letter; the person signing the letter (all capital letters), followed by the dictator's (all caps), if different, and then those of the typist (all lowercase)
- *enclosure:* indicates that additional paperwork is included in your correspondence; use the word *enclosure*, or *attachment*, placed two lines beneath the reference initials
- *filename notation:* references a file name; placed two lines beneath the last notation
- *delivery notation:* used when the document requires special handling; placed two lines below the last notation
- *cc notation:* tells your reader who else is being sent a copy; use *cc* if one or two people, or *distribution* if more. Place it flush left, two lines below the last notation
- *postscript:* P.S. at the very bottom (flush left), placed two lines below the last notation, followed by the sender's initials (use sparingly, if at all, in business correspondence)
- *continuation page:* any page after the first page of a document. Put the addressee's name, the date, and the page number at the top left corner of each page, flush left.

• Formatting Guidelines

1. Traditional
   subject line—two lines below salutation
   body—begins two lines below salutation or subject line
   first line of each paragraph—indented five spaces to right
      of left margin
   signature—four lines below closing
   company signature—four lines below closing
2. Semi-block
   subject line—two lines below salutation
   first line of each paragraph—indented three spaces
   signature—four lines below closing
   company signature—four lines below closing
3. Block
   subject line—two lines below salutation
   body—begins two lines below salutation or subject line
   signature—four lines below closing
   company signature—four lines below closing
4. Full-block
   date line—at left margin
   subject line—two lines below salutation
   closing—at left margin
   signature—four lines below closing
   company signature—at the left margin, four lines below
      closing
5. Square block
   date line—on same line as first line of inside address, but
      at right margin
   subject line—two lines below salutation
   signature—four lines below closing
   company signature—four lines below closing
   sender's and typist's initials—on same line as company
      signature line
6. Simplified
   salutation—omit
   subject line—three lines below inside address

body—begins three lines below inside address or subject line

closing—omit

company signature—five lines below body of letter

• GOOF-PROOF SAMPLES •
BUSINESS LETTERS

• Traditional Letter Format

Gainesville Board of Education
591 Lake Haven Drive
Gainesville, FL 32604

September 19, 2003

Abraham Lincoln High School
Attention: Holly Martin, Principal
12 King Street
Gainesville, FL 32604

Dear Ms. Martin:

RE: Custodial Update

On Monday, the night custodians will begin waxing all classroom floors. Please inform your teaching staff. I am working with the Registrar's office to head off conflicts with evening class schedules, which should be minimal.

In order to wax the floors, all furniture will have to be removed from the rooms, so please remind teachers to clean off the tops of their desks and to take anything of value home with them until Wednesday morning, when the waxing will be completed.

Thank you for your cooperation.

Sincerely,

Audrey Lipton
Supplies Manager

AL/bc

• Semi-Blocked Format

PATTERSON DESIGNS
123 Langston Drive, Suite 102, New York, NY 10007
TEL (212) 555-2245 FAX (212) 555-5346
www.pattersondesigns.com

December 12, 2003

Mr. James McFarin
Brilliant Ideas, Inc.
149 Hill Street
Long Island, NY 10456

Dear Mr. McFarin:

RE: Office Makeover

    It was a pleasure meeting with you yesterday morning, and I believe the new design scheme that we discussed will complement the existing décor, carpeting, and interior architecture of your office. I have already ordered the eggplant loveseat, armchair, and ottoman you selected, and they should arrive within the month.

    Unfortunately, the fabric we chose for your curtains is incredibly popular and, consequently, my distributor is currently out-of-stock. However, he has assured me that the fabric will be available in six to eight weeks. The late arrival of the fabric may delay the estimated completion date of February 1 by two weeks or more. If such a delay is unsatisfactory, please let me know, and we can select another equally suitable fabric at your earliest convenience.

Sincerely,

Sylvia Patterson

SP/ck

• Blocked Format

Kim Lang
Restaurant Supply Source
16 East Elm Street
(444) 555-1234
klang@rss.com

November 2, 2003

Jamie Chadjurjian
Howell's Fine Dining
55 5th Street
Newton, CT 06001

Dear Jamie:

RE: Bakeware Line

I have looked into the line of bakeware you mentioned during our phone conversation yesterday. The manufacturer of the pans you are interested in assures me that they can be made in the 14 x 20 size you requested. They can be ordered in either a plain stainless finish, or with a non-stick coating.

You can view both types of pans at www.webakewell.com/pans. Please let me know at your earliest convenience which type you prefer. I will also need to know how many you would like to order.

When I get this information from you, I will request prices and a delivery schedule. Thank you for your continued business. I look forward to helping you.

Yours truly,

Kim Lang
CEO, Restaurant Supply Source

KL/gs

• Full-Blocked Format

PATTERSON DESIGNS
123 Langston Drive, Suite 102, New York, NY 10007
TEL (212) 555-2245 FAX (212) 555-5346
www.pattersondesigns.com

February 15, 2004

Mr. James McFarin
Brilliant Ideas, Inc.
149 Hill Street
Long Island, NY 10456

Dear Mr. McFarin:

RE: Office Makeover Completion

I am happy to report that your new curtains have arrived and will be hung in your office tomorrow morning. Thank you for being so patient about the repeated delays. I will oversee the finishing touches to your office over the next three days, and the entire project should be completed by the end of the week.

Please call me with any questions or comments. I look forward to your feedback!

Yours truly,

Sylvia Patterson
Patterson Designs

SP/hw

• Square-Blocked Format

Signs of the Times
435 Abenaki Street
Haddonfield, NJ 08033

May 16, 2003

Henry Wilson
Otter River Awnings
19 South Lake Drive
Warren, VT 05471

Dear Henry:

RE: Awning Signs

Thank you for considering our business to design and produce the signs your client has requested for her new awnings. We have done many similar projects in the past, and I know we can provide you with a product to satisfy you and your client's needs.

As you look over the attached proposal, keep in mind that it was generated using only the information provided to us by your company. If there are any further specifications from your client that were not forwarded to us, please let me know and we will incorporate them in a new proposal. Similarly, if there are any changes that you or your staff would like to see made, send me an e-mail at jbirnn@signtimes.com or call us at (860) 888-7777.

I look forward to hearing from you soon.

Sincerely,

Jane Birnn Vice President, Signs of the Times   JB/cd

• Simplified Format

Panache Styles
122 Hart Street
Campbell, IL 60000
PanacheStyles.com
606-555-9742

January 3, 2004

Gerry Berger
Turlington Textiles
905 Little River Lane
Crystal Lake, IL 62004

RE: Fabric Defect

I am enclosing a sample piece of the 300 yards of "Country Dots" we received yesterday. As you can see, there is a defect running through the fabric. As such, it is not useable.

If you have another 300 yards of the same dye lot, please let me know by the end of the week, and I will suspend production until we receive the new fabric. It is my expectation that you will forward the fabric overnight at no additional charge.

If you do not have the yardage, I will have to go through your Spring offerings again and make another selection. The defective material will be returned to Turlington either in exchange for the new 300 yards, or for a credit.

Thank you for your prompt attention to this matter. If you have any questions, please call me at the number above, or e-mail me at cbower@panachestyles.com.

Cherie Bower
Owner, Panache Styles

CB/yf

RULE #45: Get Your Memos into Shape

Written for an internal audience, your memos may be read by colleagues and superiors. Don't send out these less formal communications with formatting errors.

• GOOF-PROOF IT! •

The purpose of a memo is to serve as a short, informal, written business communication—to briefly outline a particular situation, transaction, or agreement. While letters are usually used for communicating with those outside your company, memos are for internal communication. Styles vary from one organization to another, but memos are typically less formal and less complicated in form. Study a number of memos written by superiors and other employees to determine the style accepted in your workplace.

• Formatting Guidelines

Memos have two parts: the heading and the body. The heading is comprised of four or five lines: To, From, Date, Reference or Subject line, and cc (if necessary).

To
- List the recipients of the memo. Include first and last names and titles (or departments) for more formal memos or memos to superiors. If all recipients know each other's names and positions, use just the first initial and last name of each recipient.
- When you have several recipients, list them alphabetically or by rank of position.
- If you are writing an external memo, include the name of the company that each recipient works for as well.

- If your memo is going to many people, name the group or groups that the recipients belong to (as long as everyone in that group is getting the memo).

For example:

TO: All Employees
TO: Production Managers
TO: Production Line Assistants

From

List the author(s) of the memo in the same way you listed the name(s) and/or title(s) of the recipients. If the memo is from several people, follow the same rule: List them alphabetically or by rank.

Date

List the month, date, and year just as you would in a letter (March 28, 2003, not 3/28/03 or Mar. 28th '03).

Reference or Subject Line

The reference or subject line of a memo should be very specific, while still short enough to fit on one line. For example, compare the two re: lines below:

Instead of:

RE: Workman's Compensation

Use:

RE: Changes in Workman's Compensation Benefits for Maintenance Personnel

Distribution/cc

List those readers who are not direct recipients of your message but who should have a copy for their information or reference.

Body

The body of a memo contains the rough equivalents of an introduction, body, and conclusion, but in a more condensed form than in a letter. In a memo, a clear topic sentence should immediately inform the reader of the subject under discussion. Then, depending on the purpose of the memo, continue the discussion:

- *Directly:* Begin with the most important points, add examples or details, and end with the least important point. Use the direct approach when simply relaying information.
- *Indirectly:* Argue a point, using evidence and detailed information, and work toward a conclusion. This approach works well for memos directing others toward action.

If your memo is more than a page long, you may want to consider the use of headings to organize your information. In the revision stage, note the main topics, and write short, precise phrases to summarize each one. If you made an outline before writing your memo, use it to devise headings.

Include a summary or conclusion if your memo is long enough (typically more than one page) to warrant it, or if you feel you need to reiterate your main points in a persuasive argument. If you are asking the reader to take an action, this should also be clearly stated in the conclusion.

If you need to attach another document or documents to your memo, add a line below your closing alerting the reader to the attachments. For example:

Attachment: Graph showing customer service calls received January–June 2003

● GOOF-PROOF SAMPLES ●
MEMOS

To: Liz Boyer
From: Betty Busciglio
Date: April 26, 2003
Re: Inventory Control

Liz, great job on the inventory! You exceeded my expectations, and our whole team will benefit from your work.

Enjoy your long weekend—you deserve it!

PATTERSON DESIGNS
Interoffice Memo

To: Cindy Morgan
From: Sylvia Patterson
Date: October 31, 2003
Re: New Slipcovers
Cc: Miriam Langston
           Hugh Gilmore
           Michael Josephs

Our new line of slipcovers will be available for purchase by clients on December 1 (just in time for Christmas).

Samples of our new slipcovers have finally arrived and are available for your perusal in the conference room. The covers can be made with cotton, denim, leather, raw silk, or polyester fabric and come in a variety of colors, including eggshell, ivory, sky blue, navy blue, rust, lavender, and chocolate. The cotton and polyester fabrics are also available in an assortment of designs, including pinstripes, plaid, and gingham. The final prices of all slipcovers, which have yet to be determined, will include complimentary scotch-guarding.

Please take a look at the samples before the end of the week. Your feedback is appreciated.

INTEROFFICE MEMO

TO: Elena Pierce
FROM: John Fitzpatrick
DATE: December 12, 2003

RE: Matinee Movie Theater Account

Arnold Lexington, the president of the Matinee Movie Theater chain, has several specific requirements with respect to our upcoming proposal for the company's new ad campaign.

Overall, he wants the ads to capture the old-fashioned sensibilities of early-twentieth century Hollywood films. So, all ads should be filmed in black and white, and only movies and movie stars from the 1920s to the 1950s should be referenced in the ads.

He would also like us to create a suitable mascot for the chain, possibly a talking ticket stub as well as an original jingle, which should be entirely instrumental, prominently featuring either a piano or a violin.

The rest of the details and content are up to us. Let's have a brainstorm meeting at 9 A.M. tomorrow in the conference room.

RULE #46: Write Agendas That Lead to Better Meetings

Learning the basics of agenda writing will help ensure good atten-dance at, preparation for, and timeliness of meetings.

• GOOF-PROOF IT! •

Business meetings run smoothly when they follow an agenda written and distributed to attendees in advance. An agenda out-lines the specifics of a meeting. It is distributed to all attendees in advance of the meeting, and has a number of important purposes:

- notifies or reminds participants of the meeting date, time, and place
- focuses participants on the meeting's goal
- indicates the items to be discussed
- circulates any relevant documents for perusal before the meeting
- serves as a guide for the chairperson, helping maintain focus and time control

• Formatting Guidelines

When writing an agenda, use lists rather than sentences to get information across. The sections of an agenda will vary, but may include lists of:

- attendees
- meeting specifics (when, where)
- purpose of meeting
- topics to be covered/discussion items
- summary

Make each item on your list:

- detailed and specific
- logically sequenced
- clearly labeled or numbered
- as brief as possible

• GOOF-PROOF SAMPLES •
AGENDAS

Business Solutions, Inc.
Network Technology Division
Kalamazoo, Michigan

Summary:	Meeting with Client, Incorporated
	December 12, 2003
	12:00 P.M.
	Conference Room C
Purpose of Meeting:	Review the division's reorganization with client; get feedback on what it means to them.
	Introduce new division manager, Warren Chiu.

Attendees:

Name	Organization	Title
Matt Sizlowski	BSI	Regional Sales Manager
John Mahmood	BSI	Network Technology Senior VP
Warren Chiu	BSI	Network Technology Division Manager
Gordon Smith	CI	Director of Operations
Cathy Dobbs	CI	Commodity Manager
Cynthia Lange	CI	Director of Engineering

Agenda:

Topic	Presented by
1. BSI reorganization	W. Chiu
2. Delinquent Payments	M. Sizlowksi
3. Facilitating better Communication	J. Mahmood, C. Lange

Brief Summary:
Our client has expressed concerns about reorganization and difficulties communicating with division leaders. They are particularly worried about technical support.

We need to present the reorganization positively as it relates to this client and our operations in general. We will present a new chain of command, with contact people at three levels.

Kenyon Advertising
Burlington, Vermont

Agenda for Meeting of Creative Staff and Account Managers, Homegrown
Bread account

Date: May 3, 2003
Time: 9:00 A.M.
Place: Champlain Room

Attendees:
J. Heilbrun
A. Walsh
C. Torelli
N. Lee
F. Stein

Purpose of Meeting:
Agree on common terms for dealing with Homegrown
Familiarize staff with account
Familiarize staff with new campaign
Devise strategies for dealing with feedback

Discussion items:
1. History of account
2. Presentation of Homegrown Bread campaign
3. Comments re: print and video concerns
4. Outline of pricing structure
5. Client feedback thus far

RULE #47: Professional Proposals Get Noticed

When you want to convince someone that your idea or project is a good one, write a dynamic proposal.

● GOOF-PROOF IT! ●

A proposal is a formal attempt to get action from a colleague or superior. Whether you aim to get approval, sponsorship, agreement, or support, you want to write and format your proposal to achieve the desired result. Proposals may take the form of a letter, memo, or another written business communication. Follow the Goof-Proof guidelines to get your proposal in winning shape.

No matter what the reason for writing a proposal, be sure to:

- clearly state your intentions—define your idea so that there is no room for misunderstanding
- detail appropriate background material necessary to decision making or action on topic
- be specific when making a case for your idea, and in your explanation of how you will follow through with your plan
- offer solutions to any potential problems before they are brought up
- provide step-by-step directions as to how to proceed once the proposal is accepted

● Parts of a Proposal

Depending upon the length and complexity of the proposal, these parts may not be separated as individual sections. Remember, not all parts are applicable for every proposal.

Title, Author, Date, Audience

Make sure your proposal has a simple, direct title and that it indicates the date, the author of the proposal, and the receiver. If your proposal is in memo form, this information will be taken care of in the heading of your memo and should not necessarily be repeated in the body.

Problem/Concept Statement

Describe the problem, or concept, providing sufficient background information so that readers fully understand it.

Description of the Solution

First, use a general topic sentence to summarize the solution. Then provide the specific details of the solution. Readers need to know exactly what's involved in a solution before they can approve it. You can break the solution down into the following parts:

1. *Procedures*—Use if your solution requires several steps or complicated procedures. List steps to be taken in chronological order.
2. *Personnel*—If several people will be working on this solution, explain who those people are and why they are the best ones to accomplish those tasks.
3. *Materials*—List any special equipment or materials required for your solution.
4. *Time Line*—Explain how long your solution will take (this may be an estimate).
5. *Budget*—Use if there are large costs involved and you can provide accurate figures.

● GOOF-PROOF SAMPLES ●
PROPOSALS

GRAND IDEAS
Marlett Grand Hotel
Internal memo

Submitted by: Maritza Luiz
Department/Title: Housekeeping Supervisor
Date: 8/21/03

To:Helena T. Courtside
Proposal: Spanish translation of employee manual

As you know, over half of our employees speak Spanish as their native language, and many of them have not had a formal education in English. As a result, many of them have difficulty reading our Employee Training Manual, and I spend much of my time explaining things to employees that they should have learned from reading the manual.

I propose that we translate the manual into Spanish. If we had a version of the manual in their native language, these employees would complete training sooner and have a ready reference throughout their employment. In addition, I wouldn't have to spend as much time telling employees what they should already know.

I am fluent in both English and Spanish and have an excellent command of grammar in both languages. I would be happy to take on this project. To be successful and efficient, I need a few reference books costing a total of approximately $30, a computer to work on, and approval for overtime hours. I estimate that if I work an extra hour each day, I could have the manual translated in one month's time.

MEMORANDUM

TO: Bob Howard, Payroll Manager
FROM: Alexis Dern, Line Supervisor
DATE: August 4, 2003
RE: Proposal to revise time sheets

Wage-grade employees are currently required to fill out two different
time sheets each week: one for regular hours and one for overtime
hours. This means that employees have to write their name, Social Security number, department, supervisor, and week begin/end dates on both
sheets and get two supervisor signatures. It is a small but unnecessary
waste of time that several employees in my group have complained
about.

If the time sheets were combined so that regular and overtime hours can
be reported on one form, this would no longer be a problem. Employees
could fill out their personal information at the top, their regular hours in
the middle, and any overtime hours at the bottom. A combined form
would not only save time each week, but it would also save paper. I propose we get one of our graphic designers to meet with you regarding
design specifics before creating the new combination time sheet. The
meeting should take less than half an hour, and design could be completed in a few hours. The form could be printed in-house to save on the
cost up front, but we will begin to save money immediately as half the
current amount of paper will be used by employees.

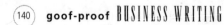

CLIENT   McMillan Downtown East Hotel
JOB   Scheduled Arrangement Supply
CONTACT   Kim Purdy
DATE   January 4, 2004

OBJECTIVES
1. To provide four arrangements per week to client that fulfill contract obligations regarding size and quality, while retaining profit margin.
2. To use new wholesaler (Atlantic Florist Wholesalers) as source of plant materials at lower cost.
3. To train an employee or employees (Jim Wells and/or Steve Kramer) to create arrangements that meet new guidelines.
4. To set up new account and train work staff by 2/1/04. Begin servicing account using new guidelines on same date.

PRICING

Description	Materials	Labor	Final Price	Profit
Foyer Arrangement	$44.00	1 hour ($23.00)	$125.00	$58.00
Front Desk Arrangement	$27.00	.75 hours ($17.25)	$80.00	$35.75
Mens/Womens Rooms Arr.	$29.00	1 hour ($23.00)	$95.00	$43.00
Job Totals	**$100.00**	**$63.25**	**$300.00**	**$136.75**

RULE #48: Details Matter in Reports

It is imperative that all facts and figures in a report be correct, and presented in a clear and thoughtful way.

● **GOOF-PROOF IT!** ●

Reports describe the outcome of an operation or a study. They are very structured, usually including all relevant statistics and information and how they were gathered. Reports are used in almost every field, for a variety of purposes. Common business report subjects include:

- employee retention rates
- production
- meetings (minutes)
- corporate improvement suggestions
- trips
- departmental or company-wide changes
- financial issues

● **The Importance of Prewriting**

Your report will benefit from time spent prewriting and organizing your findings and information. Answer the following questions, and refer to Rule #1 on page 2 to review other prewriting strategies.

1. Has anyone else been involved in your report, such as someone who helped you with your research, or attended the meeting you will report on? List them, noting how they contributed to your report.
2. What is the purpose of your report? Are you offering new information, describing a meeting or business trip, suggesting a change based on fact finding? Be specific.

3. Who is the audience for your report? Does it differ from the ideal audience (those who would benefit from, appreciate, and/or understand it best)?

4. What is the background of your subject? Has anyone else reported on it before?

5. How can you support your report? Are there facts you can gather; tables, figures, or other documents you can include or reference?

6. Describe any consequences of your research or findings.

7. What are your company's guidelines for reports? Are there sections you must include? Do they differ from those that you think should be included?

8. Are you recommending action or change based on your report? Do you have enough evidence or a strong enough argument to warrant such a recommendation?

• Formatting Guidelines

Many companies use standard report forms, eliminating the need for employees to format their reports. If your organization does not use such forms, read reports written by fellow employees to get an idea of acceptable formats and writing styles.

No matter what specific form they take, reports follow the same basic structure as a business letter: They begin with an introduction, are followed by the body of the report, and end with a conclusion and recommendations.

Introduction
Your name, the date of your report, and a title or subject description should appear at the top of your report (if using a letter, memo, or company report form, follow standard guidelines). Clearly state the purpose, subject, and summary of the report in one or two topic sentences.

Body

These paragraphs support the main idea. Be as detailed and specific as possible, focusing strictly on relaying facts. There should be no assessment or evaluation in the body of the report. If your report has a large amount of supporting data, don't include all of it in the report. Instead, *summarize* the data and include the full information or statistics as an attachment or appendix. For example, if you're reporting on all work-related accidents, you might summarize accident data and attach copies of all the accident reports.

Conclusion/Recommendations

Assess or evaluate your subject at the end of your report. What conclusions have you drawn based on your findings or experiences? Tell your audience if there is any action to be taken or if there are any recommendations based upon what you have reported. For example, in a progress report, your conclusion might present your goals for the next report period or discuss problems you've been having during this report period. An accident report might recommend changes to be made to prevent similar accidents in the future.

• GOOF-PROOF RULE OF THUMB •

When writing financial reports:

- use numbers rather than excessive text
- use visuals to make your point (charts, graphs, and tables)
- use specific percentages rather than vague statements
- use attachments (additional notes or documents) for further clarification
- use standard terminology, rather than technobabble, buzzwords, or other pretentious language

• GOOF-PROOF SAMPLES •
REPORTS

• Sample Progress Report

PROGRESS REPORT

For the week of: 11/13/03–11/20/03
Submitted by: Robert Evans
Department: Facilities

Completed:
- repaired damage to roof from weekend's ice storm (two days)
- replaced pipes under sink in men's restroom
- repaired cracks in the wall in Conference Room C
- replaced lightbulbs in hallways

In Progress:
- Painting the cafeteria (progress is slow because I am limited to the hours I can paint in there each day)

To Do (please rank in order of priority):
- install new window blinds in newly painted offices
- clean up branches and other debris from ice storm
- finish painting cafeteria

• Sample Incident Report

INCIDENT REPORT

Submitted by: <u>Matthew Thomas</u>   Date of Incident: <u>1/21/04</u>
Position: <u>Security Guard, 2nd shift</u>   Time of Incident: <u>17:18</u>
Date of Report: <u>1/22/04</u>   Location of Incident: <u>Human Resources</u>

Description of Incident:

On Monday, January 21, at 16:32, Mr. R. Turner, a former employee, signed in at the security desk. He exchanged his driver's license for a visitor pass and put his destination down as Human Resources. At 17:18, I received a call from Maria Louis, the assistant director of Human Resources. She asked me to come to Human Resources immediately because Mr. Turner refused to leave the office, which prevented her from locking up.

I left Mark Davidson on duty at the desk and reached Human Resources at approximately 17:21. When I arrived, Mr. Turner was sitting by the receptionist's desk. I told Mr. Turner that the office was closed and that he had to leave. He said he would not leave until he saw John Francis, the director of Human Resources.

Maria explained that Mr. Francis was not in that day, but he did not believe her. She said Mr. Turner was waiting because he believed he would catch Mr. Francis as he tried to leave. When I asked Mr. Turner if her statement was true, he said yes.

I told him that he could no longer sit in the Human Resources office. If he wished to wait, he could wait by the security desk, but he would be waiting until tomorrow morning. Then I asked Mr. Turner to follow me, and he did. After I escorted him to the security desk, I asked him if he wanted to wait or have his ID back. He said he'd come back later, so I returned his ID and he signed out at 17:30. After Mr. Turner left, Maria told me that he had just been fired for insubordination.

• Sample Program Evaluation Report in Letter Form

Betty Hannaford
Company Researchers, Inc.
1220 West Side Highway
Smithville, Tennessee 37166

February 22, 2004

Samuel Kingston
President, New You Fitness
15 Shady Lane
Smithville, Tennessee 37166

Re: Program Evaluation

Dear Mr. Kingston:

We recently completed our evaluation of the group fitness programs offered at your health club. This report summarizes our findings.

We evaluated four critical areas of your programs: diversity of offerings, client satisfaction, instructor satisfaction, and cost/benefit. Group fitness, as you know, scored highest in cost/benefit. A large percentage of your gross profit comes directly from these classes. However, we did find room for improvement in both diversity and instructor satisfaction. While your clients are generally happy with the program, there was dissatisfaction among your employees, which may be directly linked to the lack of diversity in class offerings. I will address the findings in each area below; the data we collected is attached.

The lack of diversity in class offerings was cited as a problem by 42% of your instructors, and 38% of class participants. Instructors feel their talents could be better utilized by teaching new and different formats. For example, two instructors are certified in Pilates, but no classes are currently offered. In addition, your two largest competitors, Ace Gym and Body Works, both schedule spinning and Yoga classes throughout the day. Both types of classes are very popular, and well attended. More diverse offerings could expand your client base, and improve job satisfaction rates for instructors.

Diversity: Grade B

Client satisfaction is high, especially in light of the findings cited above. 81% of step aerobics students gave a "very good" rating to both instructors and class content. 76% of all group fitness participants gave a "very good" rating in terms of the health and fitness benefits they receive through attending classes. In addition, you enjoy a high percentage of participation: Of the 2,482 members currently enrolled, 72% attend a class at least once a week.

Client Satisfaction: Grade A

Instructor satisfaction could be improved in a number of areas. First, many instructors wrote that they receive higher hourly wages at other clubs in the area. Second, the scheduling of mandatory meetings on weeknights was cited as a hardship. And third, a full 90% of instructors feel they do not have the support of management when trying to obtain continuing education credits. Other areas' clubs do reimburse their employees for attendance at continuing education classes and seminars.

Instructor Satisfaction: Grade C

As expected, the cost/benefit analysis of your group fitness programs gave excellent results. Full numerical breakdowns are given in the attached data sheets, but can be summarized as follows: For expenditures of less than $75,000 per year, your program nets more than triple that amount. It is by far the best revenue generator of your facility, and every effort should be made to maintain and improve group fitness.

Cost/Benefit Analysis: Grade A

In closing, we find your group fitness program to be in good shape. There are flaws, which can be corrected without making major changes to your business model. If these corrections are implemented, you could enjoy even greater revenue from this already highly profitable segment of your business.

Sincerely,

Betty Hannaford

Company Researchers, Inc.

RULE #49: Thank You Letters Are Good Business

In order to keep your business relationships positive, make it a habit to thank those who have helped you in any way. A well-written, professional thank you letter isn't just polite—it's mandatory for good business.

● GOOF-PROOF IT! ●

When you write to thank someone, you are often reiterating something you have already said in person or on the phone. By sending a written communication, you're showing that your sentiments are sincere enough for you to take the extra time and effort to put it in writing.

Because a thank you letter is simply a specific sub-genre of the business letter, the same formatting guidelines apply. Choose a letter format to suit the formality level of the situation.

● When You Must Write a Thank You Letter

- following an interview
- after a networking meeting
- in response to any business situation where you have been given assistance
- after someone has purchased something from you

● GOOF-PROOF CHECKLIST ● THANK YOU LETTERS

✓ Literally say "thank you," preferably in the first sentence.
✓ Use company letterhead if writing to a business associate. If you know the person well, handwrite a thank you letter on personal stationery.
✓ Never use your current company's letterhead to communicate with a potential employer via the thank you letter. Use your personal letterhead or handwrite a note.

✓ Be specific about what you're thanking the person for. Use exact names, dates, places, and so on.

✓ Explain why you're grateful; mention what the person did or gave that deserves special thanks.

✓ Get to the point, and be brief.

✓ If you know the recipient well, your message should be more personal.

✓ Send it quickly. While any message of thanks is better than none, a thank you should be sent within a day.

• GOOF-PROOF SAMPLES •
THANK YOU LETTERS

Mary Ellen Bednar
Seating Unlimited
5699 Crawford Circle, Suite 801 Atlanta, GA 30456
TEL (404) 555-1238 FAX (404) 555-1239
www.seatingunlimited.com

September 15, 2003

Harold Ramsey
Ramsey Auto Company
345 Bedford Lane
Atlanta, GA 34567

Dear Mr. Ramsey,

Thank you for requesting information about the workbench stools. We are proud of our wide selection and affordable pricing. Our most recent catalog is enclosed. Should you wish to order from us, you can expect to receive shipment within 2–4 weeks. Please let me know if you have any other questions or if I can be of further assistance. I look forward to your order.

Sincerely,

Mary Ellen Bednar
Vice President, Seating Unlimited

Enclosure.

Jackson Cressey
Auto Masters, Inc.
1650 Rockford Boulevard, San Diego CA 92182
TEL (858) 555-9889 FAX (858) 555-9899
www.automastersinc.com

November 10, 2003

Mr. Lee Singh and Mrs. Rita Singh
664 Warner Street
San Diego, CA 92182

Dear Mr. and Mrs. Singh,

On behalf of Auto Masters, Inc., I would like to thank you for purchasing your new automobile at our downtown showroom this weekend. Our goal is for you to be satisfied with your purchase for the life of your car, and we will do all that we can to achieve your satisfaction.

We offer full servicing of your automobile under the warranty, and assure you that our parts and labor rates are among the lowest in the county. In addition, we would like to provide you with our VIP service free of charge for one year. This service entitles you to complimentary oil changes every 3,000 miles, one complete detailing job, and preferred scheduling for any required maintenance or repairs. Further details about our VIP service are included in the attached brochure.

For your convenience, our customer service department will be happy to set up a reminder service for routine maintenance of your vehicle. Once established, you will receive a phone call or e-mail reminder one week before a routine maintenance visit is required. To make scheduling more simple, you may schedule appointments either via e-mail or telephone.

Please take the time to carefully read your owner's manual and attached information regarding routine maintenance and our VIP service. If you have any questions, or are not completely satisfied with your new auto-mobile, please call me directly at 555-9236. I will personally see that all of your needs are quickly and thoroughly met. Auto Masters, Inc. is here to serve you.

Sincerely,

Jackson Cressey
AutoMasters, Inc.

JC/kl

Enclosures.

RULE #50: Be Precise When Writing Instructions or Directions

It's important to be clear and specific when writing instructions. No matter what the instructions are for—applying for a loan, installing software, or operating machinery—they must be understood clearly by the reader.

• GOOF-PROOF IT! •

Leave nothing to chance when it comes to writing instructions and directions. Don't use words that can be misinterpreted. Keep the language simple and straightforward. Break everything down into simple steps, separated into a numbered or bulleted list. Even if adults will use the instructions, they should be written and formatted so that a sixth grader could understand them.

• Audience

The first step in writing a set of instructions or explaining procedures should be familiar to you by now: *Identify your audience.* Who will be reading these instructions or procedures? What do these readers need to know, and why? At what level of technicality or familiarity should you be writing to those readers?

Your instructions will be most successful if you determine your audience's *"lowest common denominator"* of knowledge. If all readers know A, most know B, and only some know C, you can't write to the level of B or C—you *must* write to level A. If you don't, those readers who know A but don't know B or C will not be able to follow your directions.

It's okay to risk wasting your readers' time by telling them things they may already know. Readers will skip over what's familiar, quickly separating new information from old. Never omit anything that someone *may not* know.

• Be Thorough

When writing instructions or directions, be as thorough as possible. With your lowest common denominator in mind, list and explain every step of the process for someone at that level.

For example, imagine you got a new coffee machine in your employee lounge and wanted to write directions for its use. Most readers, you might assume, have a coffee machine at home, but you can't be sure. Perhaps there are one or two people who don't. Maybe some people only drink tea and have never used a coffee machine. Thus, the lowest common denominator—the level to which you must write—is made up of people who have *never* used a coffee machine before. Don't leave out any step in the process. Your goal is to be thorough enough so that everyone who reads them achieves the desired end result.

• GOOF-PROOF CHECKLIST •
INSTRUCTIONS AND DIRECTIONS

In addition to being written for the right audience, good instructions are also easy to follow. Here are a number of strategies to help you write such directions:

✓ "Signpost" Your Readers—Let your readers know that they're doing things right. For example, *"Take Route 1 to Main Street"* is not nearly as helpful as the following:

Take Route 1 five miles (approximately 10 minutes) to Main Street. Look for the YMCA on your left; Y Street is the next intersection after the YMCA. (If you pass the gas station, you have gone too far.)

✓ Use Lists—Lists are easier to follow than straight narrative. Use separate paragraphs for each step, and, if possible, number or letter those paragraphs or set them off with bullets. It's also crucial to list the steps in *chronological order*. Steps in a list that are out of order will confuse, maybe even endanger, readers.

✓ Use Specific Information—Use exact names and numbers (times, distances, sizes, etc.) whenever possible. If you are vague, your readers may have trouble understanding. For example, "Submit your evaluations to Human Resources" is not nearly as clear as "Submit your evaluations to Deana Brown in Human Resources, Room 112."

✓ Use Warnings—You can help your readers and make your directions much safer by providing warnings or cautions when appropriate. For example, "WARNING: If the valve is not in the OFF position, pressure buildup may cause the pipe to burst."

● GOOF-PROOF RULE OF THUMB ●

When writing instructions:

- Always make sure you thoroughly understand a procedure before you attempt to write about it. If you don't, you drastically increase the likelihood that you will leave something out or make a mistake in order.
- Get feedback. This is the best way to ensure that what you have written does what it's supposed to do.
- Follow your own instructions. Don't do what you know how to do; do only what you have written, exactly how you have written it. Does it work? If not, revise. Then show your instructions to someone else, preferably someone who has never done the task you're explaining. Are your instructions clear? Easy to follow? Complete? See if your reader can perform the task without any trouble.

● Formatting Guidelines for Instructions and Directions

As with many other business writing formats, instructions generally have three parts: an introduction, a body, and a conclusion.

1. Introduction

   All instructions should have some sort of introduction. For a short set of instructions, all you really need is an explanation of what the instructions are for: "How to clear a paper jam" or "Procedure for clearing paper jams," for example.

   If your instructions are more detailed, or if there's a particular reason why people should follow these instructions, then an introduction should also tell readers *why the instructions are important*. For example, you might get a memo from payroll with the following introduction:

   > Here are the procedures for completing and submitting time sheets. It is essential that you fill out the sheets properly. Errors on these sheets will mean errors on your paycheck. Be sure to fill out each sheet completely. Incomplete sheets will not be processed.

   This introduction offers important information that will help readers follow the procedures more carefully. Introductions for instructions may also:

   - indicate how long the procedure will take
   - describe what the finished product should look like
   - mention a particularly important item that might be overlooked or that needs to be emphasized (e.g., "Be sure to pay particular attention to the deadlines listed below.")
   - list any materials that the reader may need to follow the instructions—forms, tools, etc.

2. Body

   The body of a set of instructions lists the specific steps of the procedure *in chronological order*. It can vary greatly in length depending on how much information is needed to follow the instructions.

3. Conclusion

   A brief conclusion is often helpful for telling readers:

- whom to call if they have any trouble
- what to expect next or from the results
- how to follow up, if necessary, on the procedure (e.g., "If you do not receive a reimbursement check within three weeks, contact Ms. Miller in accounting at extension 345.").

● GOOF-PROOF SAMPLES ●
INSTRUCTIONS

Procedures for Tuition Reimbursement:

All full-time employees are eligible for tuition reimbursement for undergraduate course work towards an AA, BA, or BS degree or graduate coursework that is work-related. To receive reimbursement for tuition expenses, **you must submit a completed application form to Human Resources *before* you register for class.** In addition, you must earn a 'B' or better in the class in order to be eligible for reimbursement. Detailed instructions follow:

1. Get a Tuition Reimbursement Application Form from Debbie in Human Resources.
2. Fill out the form *completely.* Incomplete forms cannot be approved.
3. Have your supervisor sign the bottom of the form.
4. Make a copy of the completed form to keep for records. You will need this form to pick up your reimbursement.
5. Submit the original completed application to Lorraine in Human Resources. Human Resources must have this form on file before you register for the course.
6. Register for and complete the course you were approved to take.
7. When you receive your grade report for the course, take it to Jennifer or Andrew in payroll along with a copy of your completed application.
8. Request a Reimbursement Receipt form. Indicate on this form whether you want to be reimbursed by separate check or have the amount added directly to your payroll check. Give this form, your grade report, and your application form to Jennifer or Andrew for processing. (You should make a copy of all forms for your own records before submitting them to payroll.)

If you complete all of these steps, you should receive your reimbursement check in the next payroll period. Please call Lorraine in Human Resources at extension 4488 if you have any questions about the procedure.

To: All Teachers
From: Student Services

On September 8, our school will follow new guidelines regarding students' taking of medications while school is in session. It is imperative that all school employees both familiarize themselves with the new guidelines, and help parents and students to understand and follow them. Attached are the new guidelines. Please read them, and then proceed as follows:

1. Retrieve copies of "Medication Guidelines for Students" handouts from the office.
2. Distribute handouts on September 5 for students to take home and have signed over the weekend.
3. On Monday, September 8, collect signed handout tear-off sheets, tally, and return to the office, placing them in the special "Medication Guidelines" file.
4. Send home another handout with those students who did not return a signed sheet on September 8.
5. On September 9, return any additional signed sheets, and make a list of any outstanding sheets. Place the list in the principal's mailbox before the end of the school day.

Your cooperation in this important matter is greatly appreciated.

If you have any problems or questions, please bring them to the attention of Mary King in Principal Wiley's office (extension 16).

● PUTTING IT ALL TOGETHER ●

Each type of written business communication has its own rules. A letter shouldn't look like a memo, nor should a report be mistaken for a proposal. The key to writing effectively at work is understanding the composition and formatting differences between the eight major workplace communications.

E-mails
- may be misinterpreted if not worded correctly; there is no tone of voice, as in a phone call, to help convey your message
- feel informal, but should still be businesslike
- should be brief; if longer than a screen length, might be better as a letter or memo

- have a subject line that should be used to describe content of e-mail in as few words as possible

Basic Business Letters
- are used for correspondence with other companies; rarely used for internal communications
- document certain necessary information (who wrote to whom, when, and about what)
- organize information neatly
- help readers find information quickly through a standard, recognizable format

Memos
- are shorter, less formal, and less complicated in form than letters
- are used for internal business communication
- should include headings if longer than one page

Agendas
- notify participants of meeting time, place, and topic(s)
- guide chairperson through meeting, helping maintain focus and time control
- should be detailed, specific, logically sequenced, clearly labeled, or numbered

Proposals
- formally attempt to convince someone to act on a project or idea
- may take the form of a letter, memo, or other written business communication
- clearly and specifically state intentions and explanation of follow-through
- offer solutions to any potential problems before they're brought up
- provide step-by-step directions as to how to proceed once accepted

Reports

- follow same basic structure as business letter
- describe the outcome of an operation or a study
- benefit from time spent prewriting and organizing findings and information
- are very structured, usually including all relevant statistics and information
- end with conclusions and any necessary recommendations
- should summarize supporting data and include full information or statistics as attachment or appendix

Thank You Letters

- say "thank you," preferably in the first sentence
- are brief, succinct, and specific about what you're thankful for
- should be sent immediately

Instructions/Directions

- must be absolutely understood by the reader, and as thorough as possible
- should be tested for effectiveness
- must be written to the lowest common denominator

section **SEVEN**

RESOURCES

appendix **A**

USING COMPUTER FORMATTING, GRAMMAR, AND SPELLING TOOLS

● COMPUTER FORMATTING IN MICROSOFT WORD ●

Microsoft Word allows you to set everything from paragraph indentation to the look (font style and size) of different types of text.

Simply:

1. Click on "Format" on the toolbar.
2. Click on "Style."
3. Find the "List" box.
4. Click on "All Styles."
5. Scroll through the styles listed to find the item you wish to change.
6. Highlight the item by clicking on it.
7. Click on "Modify."
8. Click on "Format."
9. Choose what you would like to change (font, paragraph, etc.).
10. Make changes.

11. Click on "OK."
12. Click on "OK."
13. Click on "Apply."

• COMPUTER GRAMMAR TOOLS •

You should always use a grammar check program on your writing. Grammar check can find possible errors, draw your attention to them, and suggest corrections. The settings on these programs may be changed to check for only those elements that you specify; check for specific styles of writing, such as formal, standard, casual, and technical; and check for errors as you type, or when you are finished.

To modify the grammar check settings in Microsoft Word, open a blank document and:

1. Click on "Tools" on the toolbar at the top.
2. Select "Options."
3. Click on the "Spelling and Grammar" tab.
4. Click on "Settings" in the lower grammar section.
5. Read the list of options, and select those you want grammar check to look for.
6. Click on "OK."

Although you should always use grammar check, you should not always trust it. Grammar programs make mistakes, both by missing errors, and by flagging "errors" that are actually correct. In fact, there have been a number of studies done comparing the effectiveness of various programs, and they perform about the same (fair to poor).

The first problem, missing errors, is illustrated by the following examples. A grammar check on the following sentence did pick up the subject/verb agreement error (*I is*), but did not notice the participle error (*I studying*).

"I is ready to take the exam after I studying my notes and the textbook."

Similarly, the punctuation problems in the following sentence were not flagged.

"The recipe, calls for fifteen ingredients and, takes too long to prepare."

When grammar check does highlight an error, be aware that it may in fact be correct. But if your knowledge of grammar is limited, you won't know whether to accept grammar check's corrections. To further complicate matters, you may be offered more than one possible correction, and will be asked to choose between them. Unless you are familiar enough with the specific problem, this may be no more than a guess on your part.

While there have been improvements in computer grammar checking, nothing is more effective than a careful review of your writing after using the program. Our list of proofreading tips on page 100 offers a number of great suggestions.

• USING COMPUTER SPELL CHECKERS •

You should always use your computer's spell check function because it's fast and easy, and it catches many spelling mistakes and typos. But you should also be aware of spell check's two most important limitations, and use other reliable methods to catch the errors that spell check cannot.

• Non-Word versus Real-Word Errors

Although your computer spell checker will flag strings of letters that do not make real words, it will *not* flag spelling errors or typos that *do* result in real words. For example, spell check will alert you if you mistakenly type *gorila* instead of *gorilla* or *becase* instead of *because*. But it won't alert you if you mean to type *and* but type *an* instead because *an* is a legitimate word; it's just not the word you meant to type. Likewise, spell check won't flag errors that result from commonly confused words, such as typing *to* when you meant to type *too* or *two*.

• Proper Nouns

The dictionary that spell check uses does not include most proper nouns and may also exclude technical and field-specific terms. If spell check doesn't recognize a word that you know is spelled correctly, verify the spelling using another reliable source, then simply add it to spell check's dictionary.

appendix **B**

ONLINE RESOURCES

• BUSINESS WRITING TIPS & STRATEGIES •

www.basic-learning.com/wbwt/tips-index.htm—Bull's Eye Business Writing Tips

www.business-letter-writing.com—Secrets to Effective Business Letter Communication

www.bigchalk.com—offers business writing tips and strategies for students

www.businessletterpunch.com—takes users through the steps of writing a successful business letter

www.mapnp.org/library/commskls/cmm_writ.htm—the Business Writer's Free Library includes general resources and advice, basic composition and writing skills resources, sample correspondence, and reference materials.

www.gailtycer.com/writing.htm—offers business writing tips

• ONLINE BUSINESS COURSES •

www.trainingbetter.com
www.learnatest.com
www.instructionalsolutions.com
www.online-learning.com/course_pbw2_desc.html
www.englishonline.net/writing/busi.html
www.onlinebusinessenglish.com

• BUSINESS TERMS •

Barron's Online: www.barrons.com
Bloomberg.com: www.bloomberg.com (includes a financial glossary at: www.bloomberg.com/money/tools/bfglosa.html)
Business Journals: www.bizjournals.com (you can personalize the site to your locality)
Business Week Online: www.businessweek.com
Career Journal from *The Wall Street Journal*: www.careerjournal.com
CNN Financial News Online: www.cnnfn.com
Fast Company Magazine Online: www.fastcompany.com
Hoover's Online: www.hoovers.com
Inc. Magazine Online: www.inc.com
Office.com: www.office.com
The Business Search Engine: www.business.com
The Wall Street Journal Online: www.wsj.com

• GRAMMAR •

www.wsu.edu/~brians/errors/index.html—Paul Brians' "Common Errors in English" site
iteslj.org/quizzes/—self study quizzes for ESL students, but useful for anyone interested in grammar
www.englishgrammar101.com—English Grammar 101. Several English grammar tutorials.

www.dailygrammar.com—Daily Grammar—offers daily e-mail messages with a grammar lesson five days of the week and a quiz on the sixth day

www.ruthvilmi.net/hut/help/grammar_help/—offers interactive grammar exercises and grammar resources

www.grammarlady.com/—offers grammar tips and features a grammar hotline

• SPELLING •

www.dictionary.com—a useful online dictionary (with thesaurus). You can sign up for "word of the day" e-mails to help expand your vocabulary.

www.funbrain.com/spell—a site designed for young people with a Spell Check spelling game

www.m-w.com—Merriam Webster Online. This site has a number of interesting features that will make you forget you are trying to improve your spelling! Check out the Word for the Wise section (www.m-w.com/wftw/wftw.htm) for fun facts about words.

www.randomhouse.com/words/—Words @ Random. Here you will find crossword puzzles, quizzes, dictionaries, and other fun stuff all in one site.

www.say-it-in-english.com/SpellHome.html—Absolutely Ridiculous English Spelling

www.sentex.net/~mmcadams/spelling.html—This site has a tricky online spelling test that is worth taking.

www.spelling.hemscott.net/—useful advice on how to improve your spelling

www.spellingbee.com/index.shtml—The Scripps Howard National Spelling Bee site contains "Carolyn's Corner" with weekly tips and information on spelling.

www.spellweb.com—This site will help you to pick the correct spelling of two versions of a word or phrase.

• LITERARY TERMS •

Glossary of Literary Criticism—www.sil.org/~radneyr/humanities/litcrit/gloss.htm
Glossary of Rhetorical Terms with Examples—www.uky.edu/Arts-Sciences/Classics/rhetoric.html
Literary Arts, Inc.—www.literary-arts.org/
Literary Criticism on the Web—http://start.at/literarycriticism
Literary Terms—www.tnellen.com/cybereng/lit_terms/
Online Literary Criticism Collection—www.ipl.org/ref/litcrit/
The Literary Web—www.people.virginia.edu/~jbh/litweb.html
Virtual Salt—A Glossary of Literary Terms: www.virtualsalt.com/litterms.htm
Wordwizard—www.wordwizard.com
Zuzu's Petals Literary Resources—www.zuzu.com

• TECHNOLOGY TERMS •

CIO Magazine Online—www.cio.com
Fast Company Magazine Online—www.fastcompany.com
Government Technology—www.govtech.net
Information Technology Association of America—www.itaa.org
National Institute of Standards and Technology—www.nist.gov
Tech Web: The Business Technology Network—www.techweb.com
Technology & Learning—www.techlearning.com
Technology Review (MIT)—www.techreview.com
Web Services Community Portal—www.webservices.org
Webmonkey—www.hotwired.lycos.com/webmonkey (especially the glossary)
Webopedia Online Dictionary for Computer and Internet Terms—www.pcwebopaedia.com/
Women in Technology International—www.witi.org

PRINT RESOURCES

● GENERAL ●

Alfred, Gerald J et. al. *The Business Writer's Handbook, 6th
Edition.* (New York: St. Martin's Press, 2000).

Bly, Robert. *The Encyclopedia of Business Letters, Fax Memos,
and e-mail.* (Franklin Lake, NJ: Career Press, 1999).

Chesla, Elizabeth. *Improve Your Writing for Work, 2nd Edition.*
(New York: LearningExpress, 2000).

Danziger, Elizabeth. *Get to the Point! Painless Advice for Writing
Memos, Letters, and e-mails Your Colleagues Will Understand.*
(New York: Three Rivers Press, 2001).

Galko, Francine D. *Better Writing Right Now.* (New York:
LearningExpress, 2002).

Iacone, Salvatore J. *Write to the Point: How to Communicate in
Business with Style and Purpose.* (Franklin Lake: Career Press,
2003).

Kirschman, DeaAnne. *Getting Down to Business.* (New York:
LearningExpress, 2002).

Kolin, Philip C. *Successful Writing at Work, 6th Edition.*
(Boston: Houghton Mifflin, 2001).

LearningExpress. *The Complete Professional: Solutions for
Today's Workplace.* (New York: LearningExpress, 2000).

Olson, Judith F. *Writing Skills Success in 20 Minutes a Day, 2nd
Edition.* (New York: LearningExpress, 2002).

Roddick, Hawley. *Business Writing Makeovers: Shortcut
Solutions to Improve Your Letters, e-mails, and Faxes.* (Avon:
Adams, 2002).

• STYLE GUIDES •

Williams, Joseph M. *Style: Ten Lessons in Clarity and Grace, 7th
Edition.* (Boston: Longman, 2002).

Strunk, William Jr. et. al. *Elements of Style, 4th Edition.* (Boston:
Allyn & Bacon, 2000).

*The Chicago Manual of Style: The Essential Guide for Writers,
Editors, and Publishers, 14th Edition.* (Chicago: University of
Chicago Press, 1993).

• GRAMMAR & SPELLING •

Devine, Felice. *Goof-Proof Grammar.*
(New York: LearningExpress, 2002).

Devine, Felice. *Goof-Proof Spelling.*
(New York: LearningExpress, 2002).

Follett, Wilson and Wensberge, Erik. *Modern American Usage: A
Guide.* (New York: Hill & Wang Publishers, 1998).

LearningExpress. *501 Grammar and Writing Questions, 2nd
Edition.* (New York: LearningExpress, 2002).

LearningExpress. *1001 Vocabulary & Spelling Questions.* (New
York: LearningExpress, 1999).

LearningExpress. *Vocabulary & Spelling Success*, 3rd Edition.
(New York: LearningExpress, 2002).

Magnan, Robert and Santovec, Mary Lou. *1001 Commonly Misspelled Words: What Your Spell Checker Won't Tell You.* (New York: McGraw-Hill Professional Publishing, 2000).

Morrow, David. *DK Pockets: Spelling Dictionary.* (New York: DK Publishing, 1998).

O'Conner, Patricia T. *Woe Is I: The Grammarphobe's Guide to Better English in Plain English.* (New York: Riverhead Books, 1998).

Olson, Judith F. *Grammar Essentials, 2nd Edition.* (New York: LearningExpress, 2000).

Princeton Review, *Grammar Start: A Guide to Perfect Usage, 2nd edition.* (New York: Princeton Review, 2001).

Straus, Jane. *The Blue Book of Grammar and Punctuation, 7th Edition.* (Mill Valley: Jane Straus, 2001).

vos Savant, Marilyn. *The Art of Spelling: The Method and the Madness.* (New York: Norton, 2000).

Wallraff, Barbara. *Word Court: Wherein Verbal Virtue is Rewarded, Crimes Against the Language Are Punished, and Poetic Justice is Done.* (New York: Harcourt, 2000).

Walsh, Bill. *Lapsing into a Comma.* (New York: McGraw Hill, 2000).

Woods, Geraldine. *English Grammar for Dummies.* (New York: Hungry Minds, 2001).

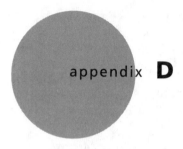

appendix **D**

ANSWER KEY

• Section 4

Rule #23: Learn the Most Commonly Confused Words, and Use Them Properly

1. I *assured* Rebecca that her new hairstyle was attractive.
2. *Their* sofa was delivered this morning.
3. The yellow dress fits better *than* the red one.
4. The *personnel* office is in the back of the building.
5. To *whom* should I address this letter?

Rule #24: Learn the Most Misused Words, and Use Them Properly

1. My brother was being indecisive, so I was forced to decide *between* the two movies.
2. After working long hours for three months, Joan was *eager* to start her vacation.
3. I lost the game but didn't *feel bad* because I'd tried my best.
4. Exhausted, she went to her bedroom to *lie* down.
5. The dinner *that* we ate last night was delicious.

Rule #25: Don't Use Words That Aren't Really Words
1. He *brought* a calculator with him to the calculus final.
2. *I hope* the meeting will go well.
3. *Anywhere* you want to meet for lunch is fine with me.
4. *Regardless* of the weather, we are going to play golf.
5. People should take responsibility for *themselves*.

Rule #26: Don't Use Words or Phrases That Might Offend Your Reader
1. The *chairperson* of our committee read a report regarding absenteeism among the *wait staff*.
2. Appropriate
3. The tennis players Venus and Serena Williams are the best in the world.
4. Please support the efforts of our Vice President of Personnel, Dora Sinclair, by sponsoring her in the Relay for Life.
5. Did you send the invitation to Dr. Choe and *Ms. Jones?*

Rule #27: Understand Positive and Negative Connotations to Choose Words Wisely
1. *Inexpensive* has a *positive* connotation. Consider *cheap* to convey the idea negatively.
2. *Encourage* has a *positive* connotation; think of it in relation to *abet*.
3. *Aromatic* has a *positive* connotation; think of it in relation to *smelly*.
4. *Ludicrous* has a *negative* connotation; *amusing* is a more positive synonym.
5. *Cozy* has a *positive* connotation (whereas *comfortable* is more neutral).

Rule #30: Formality versus Informality
Note that none of the formal words in this exercise are pretentious or archaic. You may create a formal tone with simple words that get the point across.
a. F
b. I
c. F
d. I

e. I
f. F
g. I
h. F
i. I
j. F

Rule #31: Avoid Colloquialisms

1. In conclusion, we believe you should not choose our competitor's product because they do not understand the technology the way we do.
2. The accident last Tuesday was unfortunate; we must install new floor mats to avoid another one in the future.
3. They are not sure if they will attend the meeting that we are holding tomorrow.
4. If we do not finish on time, our firm could always tell the client their last minute changes held up production.
5. The decision to cancel the trip has been made; you should accept it instead of dwelling on it.

• Section 5

Rule #35: Noun/Verb Agreement

1. Shelly and her husband *are* traveling to Spain.
2. Correct
3. Both of the managers *are* rumored to be fired after losing the account.
4. Correct
5. Either you or your brother *is* going to have to talk to your parents.

Rule #39: Double Negatives

1. We barely caught the train.
2. Lee had nothing to say at the meeting.
3. Correct
4. Heather never went anywhere on vacation.
5. Correct

Rule #40: Don't Make Spelling Mistakes

1. Incorrect—abundance
2. Correct
3. Correct
4. Incorrect—existence
5. Incorrect—fulfill
6. Incorrect—globally
7. Incorrect—harass
8. Correct
9. Correct
10. Incorrect—occasionally
11. Incorrect—parallel
12. Correct
13. Incorrect—questionnaire
14. Correct
15. Incorrect—relevant
16. Incorrect—scary
17. Correct
18. Incorrect—temperature
19. Incorrect—vacuum
20. Incorrect—wherever

Rule #41: Use Punctuation Marks Correctly

1. it's
2. its
3. It's
4. its
5. it's

Rule #42: Don't Overuse Capital Letters

1. Correct
2. Next *Wednesday* is *Dr. Lee's* lecture.
3. Do you want me to pick up the copies at the *Xerox* machine?
4. Correct
5. Make a right on Maple *St.*, and then stop in front of the post office.